DEMOCRATIC PROFESSIONALISM IN PUBLIC SERVICES

Jane Lethbridge

First published in Great Britain in 2019 by

Policy Press
University of Bristol
1-9 Old Park Hill
Bristol
BS2 8BB
UK
t: +44 (0)117 954 5940
pp-info@bristol.ac.uk
www.policypress.co.uk

North America office:
Policy Press
c/o The University of Chicago Press
1427 East 60th Street
Chicago, IL 60637, USA
t: +1 773 702 7700
f: +1 773 702 9756
sales@press.uchicago.edu
www.press.uchicago.edu

© Policy Press 2019

British Library Cataloguing in Publication Data
A catalogue record for this book is available from the British Library.

Library of Congress Cataloging-in-Publication Data
A catalog record for this book has been requested.

ISBN 978-1-4473-4210-6 paperback
ISBN 978-1-4473-4212-0 ePub
ISBN 978-1-4473-4213-7 Mobi
ISBN 978-1-4473-4211-3 ePdf

The right of Jane Lethbridge to be identified as author of this work has been asserted
by her in accordance with the Copyright, Designs and Patents Act 1988.

Cover design by Robin Hawes
Front cover: image kindly supplied by Shutterstock
Printed and bound in Great Britain by CMP, Poole
Policy Press uses environmentally responsible print partners

Contents

List of tables and figures

Tables

Figure

Acknowledgements

I would like to thank Jon Sibson and Bruce Cronin for continuing to support my research and writing, David Hall for many years of discussions about public services, public sector trade unions and the role of labour in public services, Jan Willem Goudriaan for his insights into implementing political strategies and Jill Jameson, Sian Moore, Heather Wakefield and Patrick Ainley for support in the various stages of writing this book.

I would also like to thank Policy Press and my editors Laura Vickers-Rendall and Christie Smith for steering the publishing of this book.

Preface

This book has been informed by my experiences over many years, which started with my involvement in community health campaigns against cuts in the NHS budget and more widely for improved access to health services. This was accompanied by working for voluntary organisations which I believed, then, had an important role in contributing to innovation in public services. The experience of working in the voluntary sector also gave me insights into how workers can design and run services with little overall management. This has helped me to appreciate the role of workers in designing and managing services, especially in sectors where the quality of service is directly related to the quality of the workers. Judith Tendler's book 'Good Government in the Tropics' (1997), which examined how public service workers worked to improve public service delivery in Brazil, has helped to shape my view that public service workers should guide reforms of public services.

With the introduction of public management reforms, I became intrigued by how people manage the tensions between their ideals and the requirements and practicalities of service delivery in an environment led by targets and inspections. More generally, I have seen the impact of public sector reforms on public services and the damage to public professionals working in those services.

Working for the Public Services International Research Unit (PSIRU) at the University of Greenwich for over 17 years has given me a privileged place to contribute research to public sector union campaigns against privatisation and the lobbying for improved public services at European and international levels. The importance of public service workers being well paid, trained, supported and respected remains a goal that is too rarely achieved.

More recently, in an age where experts are no longer valued, I have become interested in the concept of the professional, how it has been viewed over time, how professional identities are created and their role in the delivery of public services. Some of the reasons for the sceptical view of experts lie, I think, in a lack of democracy in the way in which expertise is created and shared. The role of professionals in the future democratic design and delivery of public services has yet to receive the attention that it merits. This book is an attempt to raise the profile of this issue.

Jane Lethbridge

1

Creating democratic public services

There is a danger that the constitutional, legal, cultural and leadership factors, which together create what is important and distinctive about public services, are not reflected on, or are dismissed as the bureaucratic problem which must be 'reformed.' (Matheson, 2002)

This book provides a set of ideas which aim to contribute to the creation of democratic public services that value service users and public service professionals so that they support and complement each and are not set against each other. It will aim to challenge the concept of provider capture, principal agent theory and other concepts used to justify public sector reforms by exploring the use of democratic approaches to public service delivery. Public services are delivered to citizens and are funded by public expenditure through taxation. They are an essential part of democracy but the degree to which democratic processes shape the delivery of public services is often limited, made more so by outsourcing and privatisation.

Public services need to be democratised in the light of changes taking place in the way in which public services are delivered, for example, increased personalisation. We need to find ways of defining the type of public services needed in future. Whereas the current emphasis in public sector reform is on how to involve service users as co-producers of services, this book focuses on the public sector professionals who deliver public services and explores how public service professionalism within public services could operate in a more democratic way. The answers may vary according to the type of public service, but there are some basic questions which all public service professionals would benefit from trying to answer.

Types of democracy

Erik Olin Wright (2010) in *Envisioning Utopias* sets out how democracy or 'rule by the people' is put into practice through three systems of democracy. As a way of exploring what a democratic professionalism might look like an outline of different forms of democracy will provide a clearer understanding of some of the processes which underpin democratic practice. Some of the forms of democracy can be defined in terms of organisational systems, structures and arrangements, whereas other forms are more normative and aspirational.

Representative democracy is a widely understood term. Citizens vote for one or more candidates to represent them in systems of government across countries, regions or localities. This can be organised as one person one vote or one person one vote which is transferred through a system of proportional representation.

Associational democracy describes the process where different types of collective or membership organisations, such as trade unions, civic groups or business organisations are involved in political decision-making and governance. This might be through government commissions or organisational representation. The establishment of government commissions to examine a political concern, for example, long-term social care, which brings together representatives from a wide range of different organisations who apply their expertise to the problem, is an example of associational democracy.

In direct democracy citizens/participants undertake 'activities of political governance' themselves. They can vote on laws and policies and take part in public hearings or public consultations where they can articulate their views on proposed plans or experiences of services. Citizens may take part in direct budgeting where they contribute to decisions about how to use funds for neighbourhood and local government (Olin Wright, 2010). Brazil has been a leading exponent of direct democracy following the introduction of a new Constitution in 1988.

Participatory budgeting allows local people in a neighbourhood to decide on spending priorities. It has been adopted by many countries. There is a growing interest in other more normative and aspirational democratic processes. One example is deliberative democracy (Ercan and Dryzek, 2015) which is based on a belief that political decisions should be the product of fair and reasonable discussion and debate among citizens. It is a normative theory and so does not explain how democratic politics are delivered, but it can allow democratic practices to be interpreted and evaluated. Deliberative democracy is often a transformative process. Wagenaar (2007) argued for the use of philosophical hermeneutics in which knowledge or understanding is a form of dialogue. In a public policy context this has implications for processes of participation, collaborative and deliberative policy making (Wagenaar, 2007: 326).

Although these forms of democracy help to understand how democratic processes can operate, they do not provide an adequate framework to democratise public services. The democratic processes which inform the way in which institutions take decisions are also part of a democratic foundation. Dewey argued that "all those who are affected by social institutions must have a share in producing and managing them" (Dewey, 1987: 218). This is an important concept to inform the development of democratic professionalism. Dewey wrote extensively about democracy in formal and non-formal settings, particularly in relation to education. Some of his ways of seeing democracy within institutions and more widely can help to explore the concept of democracy within public services. Dewey challenged the view that democracy is only seen as part of government. He argued that democracy is a "social and ethical notion" and "upon its ethical significance is based its significance as government" (Dewey, 1888: 240).

Democracy outside of government "is primarily a mode of associated living, of conjoint communicated experience" (Dewey, 1916: 93) but this depends on individuals having access to information and the "free circulation of knowledge" (Dewey, 1916: 93). Another key element of a democratic community is that there is a balance between individual and shared interests,

3

which can be seen at the heart of the challenge that the demand for personalised services within public services which are part of universal services. Democracy is also a way of being and Dewey describes it as "expressed in the attitudes of human beings and is measured by consequences produced in their lives" (Dewey, 1939: 151).

These views of democracy show that it is much more than a formal system of government. Dewey tried to explore what democracy meant in the life of institutions or organisations and this has relevance for how public services need to start viewing democracy. Some of the questions raised by Dewey's account of democracy within institutions can be used to structure an analysis of how public services can start to incorporate democracy. For example, what is the role of democratic professionals in providing access to information, helping to balance individual and shared interests and how people deal with each other? These processes can be seen in terms of the ethics of actions within public services. How does a "mode of associated living, of conjoint communicated experience" (Dewey, 1916: 101) manifest itself within a public service? What is the role of the professionals who work in public services in this process? Acting democratically is a combination of how democratic professionals interact with service users on a daily basis and identifying needs, planning and delivering to meet these needs. A more democratic approach to creating public services would allow for the changing needs of service users to be addressed. It should include the way in which teams that deliver public services work together in a democratic way.

Although there is an extensive literature on professionals and professionalism, the challenges to professional power have most often been a criticism of any professional power. There has been relatively little written about how public service professionals can operate in a democratic way. The term 'democratic professionalism' is relatively new although there have been attempts since the 1960s to make public services more user-friendly and client-focussed. In the United States a movement of 'civic professionalism' has evolved in the last two decades, predominantly in the education sector (Boyte, 2015). Higher and further education have identified a role for educational institutions to work in a civic sense with local communities, using expertise democratically, respecting local needs and taking responsibility. This can be characterised as an attempt to make educational institutions more sensitive to meeting the needs of local communities. This book will argue that other public services can take a similar approach. What is important about civic professionalism is that it draws on the concept of public pedagogy, defined as the 'processes of education' that take place beyond formal schooling. This includes citizenship within and outside schools, popular culture, informal institutions and public spaces, dominant cultural discourses and public intellectualism and activism (Sandlin et al, 2011). This is easier to justify in the education sector, where there is an obvious pedagogical goal, but can also be seen as relevant to other public services.

Why democratic professionalism is important

Albert Dzur, the author of *Democratic Professionalism* written in the context of the United States, argued that democratic professionalism needs a "fundamental shift in power relations between 'service users' and 'service providers' and may be allied to a participatory 'rather than representative' form of citizenship" (Dzur, 2004, 2008). Experts by experience are arguing that professional practices should be opened up to democratic deliberation.

The term democratic professionalism challenges the assumption underlying public sector reform that public service users can be redefined as customers. One of the main critiques of consumerism as applied to public services is that public services are not commercial services because people use them in different ways and have different needs. Choice is not necessarily a major issue for public services, but reliability and access are important. In this sense, having a choice of appointment may be important but having a hospital or school that is accessible and provides good quality services is valued more. The question of access to information and the type of information needed to make informed choices has underpinned many of the reforms to public services. The imposition of targets, league tables and inspections onto public services and public professionals has generated several levels of bureaucracy and turned the working life of public professionals into a series of administrative processes to be followed often taking away time which could be spent on direct contact with the service user. The value of these processes is beginning to be questioned, because they are pushing public professionals away from jobs which traditionally valued a public sector ethos.

Dzur (2004, 2008) examined democratic professionalism in terms of how specialist knowledge can be used in a deliberative way to solve social problems, avoiding the often technical and bureaucratic decision-making that mainly excludes citizens. He proposed 'democratic professionalism' as a way of building bridges between specialists, for example in medicine or law. Professionals may only operate a form of technocratic professionalism, which is concerned with the continued maintenance of professional power, or they may play a role in civic professionalism, analysing the "problems of democratic engagement, authenticity and integrity" (Maharg, 2009: 1), a form of democratic professionalism. Dzur (2004) argued that professionals have democratic responsibilities to facilitate the participation of citizens in a particular sphere, which are the result of particular professional practices. This relates to "commercial- or technocratic-minded professionals...vulnerable to problems of legitimacy stemming from its remoteness from the publics served" (Dzur, 2004: 3). Rather than operating as part of commercial and technocratic systems, professionals should start to work in a more collaborative and cooperative way with their clients.

The way in which professionals should start to take on this new role was outlined by Maharg (2009). Writing from the perspective of the legal profession, Maharg (2009) defined democratic professionalism as "a form of re-professionalization built around models of active and collaborative democratic change." For lawyers, the problems of democratic professionalism highlighted the dual role that legal professionals play, because they are involved in "both the creation and maintenance of rights, and in the dialogue concerning the nature of freedom in a democracy". Maharg suggested that concepts such as Dewey's education praxis and "associate life" were important in helping professionals to work in a different, more facilitating way with citizens. Dewey saw learning as experience and explored how learning, experience, participation and communication interacted. He wrote that "all those who are affected by social institutions must have a share in producing and managing them" (Dewey, 1987: 218). This is an important concept to inform the development of democratic professionalism.

Sullivan (2004) presented an alternative to the "market model of work and social organization" which was a form of "social partnerships between the public and functional groups which organize to advance social values in the interest of those they serve" (Sullivan 2004: 15–20). This is particularly relevant for professionals operating with the Welfare State, who are responsible for the creation and maintenance of public goods rather than production of profits. These professionals need to be accountable and able to participate in civic life, making their professionalism a form of civic professionalism (Sullivan, 2004). Boyte (2010) wrote about politics and public work and defined public work as "a politics of productive action by diverse agents to create a democratic way of life" (Boyte, 2011: 633). He argued that a "reintegration of states and markets into civic life" (Boyte, 2011: 633) is needed.

Whitty (2000) presented democratic professionalism as a third model of accountability for teachers, separate and different from state control and self-regulation. A form of 'democratic professionalism' would aim to demystify the nature of professional work by building alliances with students, parents and other stakeholders. This would enable the values of idealism and trust to be redefined. 'Democratic professionalism' could challenge managerialism and would be based on collaboration between teachers, parents, students and other educational stakeholders. It would lead to new work practices and more flexible ways of thinking about practice (Sachs, 2001: 159). This was a more specific reaction to the impact of managerialism on teachers and the education sector.

This was taken further, in relation to the teaching profession, by Whitty and Wisby (2006), who argued that democratic professionalism would require teachers to take responsibility for more than just their actions in the classroom. Teachers would have to be involved in the running of the school, play a role in the wider educational system, support and show solidarity or collegiality with other teachers. However, teachers would also have to recognise that the solution to social problems and wider social agendas may have to involve the subordination of professional interests, perhaps one of the most important elements of democratic professionalism.

Biesta (2015) outlined a model for a democratic professionalism which has three characteristics: a purpose (*telos*); defining the needs of clients as well as providing services; establishing the presence of authority through the transformation of relationships of power into relationships of authority. Biesta discusses these characteristics in relation to teachers and education. In terms of defining needs, he explained that education is partly about what children and students desire, but it is also about what is needed by children and students, and this requires judgements made by teachers. The process of coming to a conclusion about what is needed has to be done in a democratic way. This informs the third characteristic, which also has to be conducted within a democratic process of teachers being authorised by students.

More recently, the concept of a democratic professionalism has continued to evolve in reaction to attacks on professional power as a result of public management reform and increasingly through digitalisation. Taubman (2013) further developed the "activist identity", building on some of the principles identified by Sachs (2003). He defined the core of democratic professionalism as an emphasis on collaborative, cooperative action between teachers and other educational stakeholders, which facilitates decision making between teachers and others involved in education. In order to create an "activist identity", which could engage with stakeholders, professionals need to:

- facilitate access to ideas and information and critical reflection and evaluation;
- believe in the capacity of people (individual and collective); and
- have a concern for others, "the common good", for their dignity and rights. (Taubman, 2011: 3)

Taubman (2013) stressed the importance of promoting democratic processes, including within institutions, although he acknowledged that this would involve an extensive process of transformation. The three elements of a democratic professionalism are similar to Dewey's three requirements for democracy within institutions: access to information, helping to balance individual and shared interests and how people deal with each other (Dewey, 1987). More recent literature has refined four elements of democratic professionalism (Oberheumer, 2005; Spours, 2014; Stevenson and Gilliland, 2015; Taubman, 2013): competence, skills and knowledge; respect; integrity; and responsibility, which cover similar issues.

These elements help to define how a democratic professional might operate. Whether it is Dewey writing at the beginning of the twentieth century or Taubman and contemporaries writing a century later the importance of access to information and valuing different sources of information emerges as one of the most important elements. This has implications for how public professionals make information accessible to their students, clients or patients, but it is also about how they value the knowledge and skills that their clients have through their own experiences or learning. Valuing this expertise often makes public professionals rethink how they work with clients. The experiences and knowledge of clients can be valued more and incorporated into the delivery of public services through a greater emphasis on listening and understanding the 'life worlds' of clients.

A second element is how to balance individual and shared/ collective needs. The emphasis on consumerism and the needs of the individual promoted by public management reforms make this difficult but a process of dialogue can start to engage clients in issues that show that individual and collective needs are not mutually exclusive.

A third element of the democratic professional is questioning ways in which public professionals can solve problems. This will have to be based on a more critical perspective of professional expertise with an awareness that working collaboratively with other professionals and agencies will strengthen new ways of delivering public services. Many of these processes have already begun but need further development.

What democratic professionalism is not

At this point, it is important to be clear about what democratic professionalism is not. There are several contemporary initiatives which are trying to change the relationship between professionals and service users. Co-production is a widely used concept which has become part of public management reforms and tries to draw service users/citizens into engaging with public services. 'Engagement professionals' are trying to break down some of the barriers between service users, institutions and public professionals in higher education. There is also a movement to improve the professionalisation of those in public office. Whether civil servants should be included in this process of democratisation is also subject to debate. These initiatives will now be discussed in relation to democratic professionalism.

The concept of co-production was originally defined by Elinor Ostrom (1972) as "user involvement in the creation and delivery of public services". Ostrom (1990, 2009) wrote extensively about how communities shared common resources, which had been regulated successfully for centuries through locally developed systems whose qualities have been underestimated by governments. In common property regimes communities protect their core resource, while allowing members of the group to use it up to certain limits or using certain technology. This is achieved through complex community norms and community decision-making.

This concept of co-production was applied in the context of urban government in the United States in the 1970s and 1980s and has been influential in the context of public sector reform. In this context, co-production sought to address some of the criticisms of public services, particularly the lack of sensitivity to user needs but during a period of reduced public spending it has evolved into a focus on how citizens can contribute assets, time and expertise to public service delivery.

Loeffler and Bovaird (2016) defined co-production as "public services, service users and communities making better use of each other's assets and resources to achieve better outcomes or improved efficiency" (Loeffler and Bovaird, 2016: 1006). They distinguish co-production from public consultation and participation, because co-production focuses on joint action between citizen and public providers, whereas public consultation or public participation is more about listening and joint decision-making. Their emphasis on outcomes and improved efficiency reflect the influence of public sector reform.

One important issue that Loeffler and Bovaird highlight is how the level of analysis which researchers have used to analyse co-production results in different perceptions of the role of citizens in co-production. If the unit of analysis is a public service, the emphasis is on how the type of public service influences the type of co-production. For services which are professionally planned and designed and delivered, the contribution of the citizen is a relatively minor activity. When the unit of analysis is a public service organisation, again the emphasis is on whether co-production can improve the legitimacy of the organisation rather than seeing citizens as central to the process of public services design and delivery.

It is only when the unit of analysis moves to the household/ service users that there is a change in the perception of co-production. The citizen often views co-production as a resource intensive activity with no clear outcome, partly because it reduces their scope for involvement in self-help or other community activities. This reflects a negative view of public services and involvement in them. However, a typography of roles of co-producers show three roles:

- clients – individual value;
- volunteers – value to others; and
- citizens – service users often with social networks and/or local geographical communities.

Loeffler and Bovaird (2016) found that there was little research that looked at which public professionals are involved in co-production from the public sector.

Van Eijk and Steen (2016) explore why citizens become involved in co-production of public services. They acknowledge that the interest in co-production is motivated by budget cuts to public services and a critical view of government rather than any understanding of why citizens might be interested in co-production. They argue that only when there is a better understanding of citizen engagement can more be done to encourage collaboration between citizens and professionals. Alford and Yates's (2015) survey of citizen motivation and co-production looked at neighbourhood safety, environment and health services and identified several types of co-production. They found that co-production which was individually performed and generated high levels of private value was most popular. Group activities which generated high levels of public value were least often performed.

These analyses of co-production show that there are many different types of co-production. Citizens' motives for engaging in co-production are often more strongly related to individual, private value rather than public, community value. Perhaps the most striking finding is the small amount of research that has been done into the role of public professionals in co-production. This could be partly a result of why co-production has been promoted. It is part of a critical approach to public services which argues that with necessary budget cuts and a reduced role of the state citizens need to become involved in co-production of public services, because public expenditure is insufficient to provide the resources required. This underlying basis for co-production shows that it is part of public sector reform which is not committed to building a stronger public sector or public services but is attempting to make citizens contribute their time and resources to the provision of public services.

Several countries have a specific public policy of encouraging public participation through the development of strategic partnerships between public agencies and local communities. Engagement professionals are a new group of public professionals who are responsible for facilitating the process of public participation and deliberation. Their specialist expertise is in process rather than a specific service or issue (Escobar, 2013). Many higher education institutions have appointed public engagement professionals to strengthen relationships with local communities and businesses, contributing to making universities more outward looking and making their resources more accessible to these groups. The difference with democratic professionals lies in the focus on facilitating a democratic process rather than on delivering a public service in a democratic way. However, public engagement professionals could be a source of professional support for democratic professionals. Local authorities have a long tradition of officers tasked with working with local communities. Some of their experiences would be helpful for democratic professionals, particularly understanding some of the tensions that arise between those working with local communities and other local authority officers who do not support the issues being raised (Mayo et al, 2007).

Another group that democratic professionals should be distinguished from are professionalised politicians and civil servants. The rise of professionalised politicians can be easily separated from democratic professionals. There is extensive criticism of professionalised politicians because they lack experience which would enable them to better understand their constituents. A career which has only moved from one position within government to another does not provide experience of local communities and the way in which they live (Allen, 2013).

Whether civil servants should operate in a democratic way with public service users can be addressed by looking at some of the reforms that civil servants have undergone recently. The original conception of a civil servant in the United Kingdom was that s/he should be impartial in judgements and so, separate from political interests. Recent reforms have attempted to make civil servants more aware of the problems of implementing public policy rather than just being responsible for the formulation of public policy. This has been achieved by some civil servants working for part of their career in agencies which are separate from central government or in local government which is responsible for the implementation of public policies. This widening of civil service experience has also resulted in their exposure to the private sector. The Civil Service Code (2010) sets out four core values that civil servants should work towards. These are:

- 'Integrity' is putting obligations of public service above your own personal interests;
- 'Honesty' is being truthful and open;

- 'Objectivity' is basing your advice and decisions on rigorous analysis of the evidence; and
- 'Impartiality' is acting solely according to the merits of the case and serving equally well Governments of different political persuasions.

The emphasis is on serving government and public service but there is no acknowledgement that the interests of government might not be those of public service. This position within policy making would make it difficult for a civil servant to become a democratic professional. Part of the Civil Service Code does provide civil servants with protection, through the 1998 Public Interest Disclosure Act, if they feel that they need to disclose information in the public interest.

This section has introduced the concept of democratic professionalism, explained some of the elements of what being a democratic professional involves and outlined what a democratic professional is not. The chapter continues with a short analysis of the contemporary condition of public services.

The contemporary condition of public services

At the beginning of the twenty-first century, the future of public services is a central political issue. In many countries, there have been over 30 years of public management reforms, led by policies of market liberalisation and privatisation. The debates about which services should be public, how public services should be delivered and what service users can expect from public services, are still raging. There are several themes emerging from these debates, which are described in terms of choice, value for money and diverse providers, signs of a new language used to describe public service delivery, which has moved away from the concepts of universalism, accessibility and collective responsibility. Although there is a growing recognition that public services are essential to an equitable and socially just society, there is no consensus about how they should be delivered and who should deliver them.

In the United Kingdom, by the 1960s and 1970s, social reforms, which introduced social rights to abortion, homosexuality and divorce, led to changes in post-war society, particularly in relation to the nuclear family, which the post-war Welfare State was predicated upon. These fundamental social changes were accompanied by a sense that Britain's economic prosperity was fragile (Bogdanor, 2012) although whether this was an accurate assessment is questionable (O'Hara, 2012). This view of economic fragility, often articulated as crisis, was part of a much longer process of industrial decline combined with the loss of empire, which came to dominate British politics in the last part of the twentieth century (Leys, 1983).

The creation of publicly funded education, health and other welfare services had led to increased expectations of what these services should deliver. In education, the selection process at age 11, formalised by the 1944 Education Act, was criticised by a growing number of people and interest groups, who felt that selection was damaging to children (Simon, 1994). The Labour government elected in 1964 published the 1965 Comprehensive Circular as a response to this criticism, encouraged but which did not compel schools to become comprehensive schools (Department of Education and Science, 1965).

Initially in 1948, the demand for NHS services was expected to decline, but by 1970, the pressures were increasing, with a growing need to integrate community health services, provided by local authorities, into the NHS. Mental health services were also being criticised and advocacy groups, such as MIND, were increasingly critical of how services were delivered, especially following a series of scandals in the 1950s (Crossley, 1998).

The role of local authorities in providing a range of welfare services was expanding but their role in child protection, although also expanding, was being questioned, resulting in the creation of the Family Rights Group to represent the needs of parents of children taken "*into care*" (Family Rights Group, 2013). The increased activity of older voluntary organisations as well the creation of these new advocacy groups was partly the response to a more open social climate, where social rights were recognised, but was also a sign that public services were not meeting the needs of all service users. The Welfare State had not addressed all Beveridge's Five Giants. Poverty had not disappeared, and unemployment was rising (Moran, 2004). Together these issues started a questioning of the post-war settlement.

The 1973 oil crisis and the 1976 IMF loan are seen as two defining events which strengthened the questioning of the post-war settlement, because it was felt that public sector spending could not be maintained to meet a growing demand for public services. Up to this point, the assumption that full employment and a progressive taxation system could continue to fund public services, which underlined the post-war consensus, had been unchallenged. Influenced by the Chicago School of Economics, a monetarist approach began to dominate economic policy. This argued that long-term economic growth would be more successful if markets were allowed to run the economy rather than the Keynesian approach that promoted demand management of the economy by the state. What became known as 'neo-liberalism' became a dominant paradigm that influenced national governments across the world and underpinned a major attack on public services, stimulated the privatisation of public enterprises and the entry of the private sector into government and the delivery of public services (Stiglitz, 2000).

With the election of Margaret Thatcher in 1979, the new Conservative government started to actively question the state role in public services by arguing that the private sector should be the preferred provider of several public services, because it would be more efficient. The myth was created that the private sector was more efficient and effective than the public sector, but this was not based on rigorous evidence (New Economics Foundation, 2013). Supported by EU legislation, which was pushing for the introduction of national markets in utilities as a means of creating a Single European Market in the provision of utilities such as water, gas, electricity and telecoms (Hermann and Flecker, 2012), the Thatcher government privatised many nationalised industries which had provided utilities. The rest of the public sector was subjected to quasi-market arrangements, introducing competition into the provision of public services through the creation of internal markets in the public sector (Flynn, 2007; McLaughlin et al, 2002). This approach was strengthened by Thatcher's successors, John Major and Tony Blair.

In this brief discussion of how the role of the state has changed since 1945, two significant terms emerge: the public sector and public services. As a result of public management reforms, public services are now delivered by a range of providers from the public, for-profit, and not-for-profit sectors. The way in which public services are delivered is the result of a contract specification set out by the commissioners of public services. There is a greater bureaucratic control of the public services through targets, inspections, monitoring, league tables and quality standards. This was facilitated by the use of information and communications technology. However, the quality of public services does not necessarily reflect the intensity of audit systems because the impact of targets and systems of monitoring can result in skewed forms of delivery, when the services are no longer viewed in a *'joined up'* way but as a series of activities to meet government targets. The voice of the user is only heard in a limited way through consumer satisfaction surveys.

Part of the process of marketisation was the introduction of the language of consumerism, including choice, the creation of league tables to enable consumers to make choices and new quality standards. Yet, although new systems attempted to empower consumers, research showed that the private sector model of consumer choice did not encapsulate what public service users wanted.

Whereas choice may inform a retail purchase, what public services deliver is the solution to a problem. An ill patient wants to be treated at the best hospital or with the best services available. Being able to choose between hospital A and hospital B is not important when someone might die.

Issues of choice in the schools' sector are slightly different but the core issue is that a student should be able to go to a good school wherever they live. In social care, the promotion of individualisation, which is a response to changing demands for care and how it is delivered, has been accompanied by the fragmentation and privatisation of care services. The use of the more superficial measures of retail consumerism, for example, choice and range of products, are not necessarily appropriate for public services.

Another important concept that informed public management reforms, was public choice theory, originally propounded by Tullock (1965), which argued that public sector workers do not work for the public interest; rather, through a process of professional capture, self-interest is the driving force of politics and bureaucracies (Neiman and Stamborough, 1998; Zafirowvski, 2001). Political parties make promises to obtain votes; politicians make deals to secure support; and bureaucrats want to maximise their own interests in terms of jobs and budgets. Le Grand (2006) saw public sector providers of public services as motivated by bureaucratic procedures, rules and regulations, rather than the interests of service users. Public choice theory provided a theoretical framework for a direct attack on the public sector workforce. Coupled with a belief that the private sector would be more effective and efficient in delivering public services, public management reforms introduced fundamental changes for public sector workers through the contracting out of services, often followed by privatisation or long-term outsourcing.

The criticisms of public services in the 1970s and 1980s, which triggered the introduction of public sector reforms, were based on the perceived inability of the public sector to meet the changing needs of citizens. The lack of a democratic dimension to public services was a weakness of the Welfare State (Todd 2014) as, too often, they relied on the unquestioned expertise of existing elites. Effective co-production or co-management of services requires the creation of relationships between service providers and service users which are not just another superficial layer of consumerist response.

Effects of reforms on the public sector workforce

Public management reforms have impacted upon many kinds of public services in England, which has affected their workforces differently. The public service utilities, for example, energy, water, telecoms, now operate as networked industries, with wholesale and retail forms of organisation, dependent on piped infrastructure. They were fully privatised by the 1990s and are now subject to regulation, the responsibility of regulatory agencies created by the state. The workforce of the major utilities, such as water, energy and telecoms, was immediately affected by the privatisation of these services because there were reductions in the numbers of workers as well as long-term changes to pay, terms and conditions (Hermann and Flecker, 2012). A second group of public services can be defined as labour intensive public services, such as schools, health services, social welfare and public administration, where the quality of services is strongly determined by the quality of labour. Health, social services and education account for at least a quarter of public spending (Pollitt, 2004).

For labour intensive public services, public management reforms have been felt in terms of corporatisation of public sector institutions, which has changed the way in which the labour force is organised, often with a slower process of outsourcing and privatisation. The rationale for public management reforms has been to improve the effectiveness and efficiency of the public sector, through the use of private sector business systems. Buchan and Ball (2011) observed that professionals within the NHS have been affected by changes in staffing, organisational culture and human resource management, but not yet by reforms to pay. Continuing austerity since 2010 and a pay cap of 1% since 2010 is affecting the quality of services and the ability of public sector professionals to operate.

The public professionals working within these labour-intensive services have some influence on how services are designed because they deliver them directly. Yet, since the introduction of public management reforms in England after 1979, the position of several professional groups, for example, teachers, nurses and social workers, responsible for delivering labour intensive public services, has undergone extensive change. It has affected not only the pay of workers but also their pensions, work pressure, casualisation, increasingly mechanistic work practices and the removal of the 'emotional' content from jobs. This can be seen in terms of daily professional practice, professional training and status. These groups have been subject to extensive criticism by government for not delivering high quality services and reforms to their professional practice have been implemented as a way of improving public service delivery. This impacts the collective ability of a teaching, social work or ward team to democratise their practice.

Steijn (2002) argued that human resources management has been a neglected subject in the debates about public management reforms, although these changes have had a direct influence on the professional groups working within these public services. They have found that the demands of markets and competition may directly challenge their professional decisions (Garrett, 2009). Ball (2008), drawing on Butler (1988), uses the term *"performativity"* to describe the new working environment in which public sector workers now operate. This is characterised by professionals working towards targets and being subject to performance reviews and appraisals.

Since the 1980s the model of 'public service professionals' who were trusted to work for clients has been challenged, with the state taking a more critical view of them (Whitty, 2000). The introduction of public management reforms has undermined this model and there is much wider questioning of the integrity of teachers and other 'public service professionals'. The breakdown of trust led to the questioning of the Welfare State and the introduction of further public management reforms. It has since become a dominant issue in the delivery of public services. However, it is not simply about whether clients and service users trust public service professionals. The supposed loss of trust has become a tool used by the state to challenge and often undermine 'public professionals'.

The introduction of managerialism through public management reforms has frequently had a negative impact on the trust relationships that professionals develop with clients. Although trust is part of the new public management discourse, it is an instrumental approach to trust in an institutional setting, rather than a more communicative model of trust between patient and professionals (Brown, 2007). However, in a study which analysed data from OECD countries, Van de Walle et al (2008) found that the trust of citizens in the public sector tended to fluctuate but there was no long-term decline in trust.

Professional work following public management reforms is defined by a series of managerial targets. These are which are measured through audits and quality monitoring, often creating a sense of distrust between professionals and managers. Although the instrumental approach to trust makes the use of a communicative model of trust between public and professionals less likely, Gilbert (2005) viewed the tensions between trust and managerialism as signs of a struggle for professional autonomy within managerial controls.

Avis (2003) argued that new teacher professionalism is based on the "teacher as a trusted servant rather than an empowered professional teacher" (Avis, 2003: 329). The teacher, as a servant, has to do what is prescribed through targets, monitoring and auditing, rather than making choices and professional decisions. Performance management thus comes to play an important part in influencing how a teacher should function. This is a conditional form of trust. As with the NHS, a wider and more expansive form of dialogue with different groups involved in education would result in a stronger and more expansive professionalism than one defined by performance management (Avis, 2003).

In a 2011 NASUWT survey, 63% of teachers felt that they were not managed in a way that empowered them professionally to deliver the best outcomes for pupils. Respondents identified several factors that contributed to their disempowerment. The most often mentioned factors were related to a lack of respect, lack of understanding of everyday teaching, a culture of blame and "punitive accountability".

Table 1: Main factors contributing to disempowerment of teachers

Factors	Response rate %
Constant change	73
Culture of blame/criticism rather than praise	60
Lack of understanding by decision makers of the day-to-day realities of the job	62
Lack of respect for teachers' professional judgement	60
Punitive accountability (e.g. external/internal inspections/moderations/league tables)	53

Source: NASUWT, 2011: survey

Teaching is considered by several teaching union leaders as "a craft but also an art and a science". Reforms have made it less of an art or a science and more of a craft. A teacher trade unionist felt that:

> Teaching isn't a craft but a reflective process which needs a theoretical understanding which can be gained from University....Need time released in schools, reflective teachers to talk together about teaching" and other measures such as a Master's degree or a term at University to reflect on practice. A PGCE doesn't solve what teachers do because training has to be continually updated. (Lethbridge, 2015: 182)

With more teachers being trained in schools, the emphasis is on dealing with immediate teaching rather than developing long term professional practice. The expansion of the school workforce, which includes teaching assistants and other less qualified support staff, is seen as a form of de-professionalisation or even proletarianisation aimed at reducing costs of the school workforce (Ainley, 2016). In the long term, the costs of education will have been reduced through reforms to the workforce. This will make it easier to privatise parts of the school system.

> School Direct may make school teaching into a craft. There is lots of money in education, you can pay teachers a lot less if they just have to ...work through worksheets and websites so why bother with a university education. (Lethbridge, 2015: 182)

The results of a Royal College of Nursing (RCN) Safe and Effective Staffing survey in 2017, which received 30,000 responses, showed how austerity was having an effect on the quality of care provided by nurses. A short fall was reported by 55% in planned staffing and 20% registered nurses were temporary. 36% of the 30,000 respondents said lack of time meant 'care undone' and over half of respondents (53%) were sad or upset at not being able to give the full care that they felt patients needed. An RCN Members' survey in 2017 found that many nurses were anxious about their financial position and were thinking of leaving their jobs. Seventy per cent felt financially worse off and 24% were thinking of leaving because of financial worries, while 37% of respondents were looking for a new job and 61% felt the pay ban was inappropriate.

In 2008, a Social Work Taskforce was set up in response to the Baby P case to look into the future of child social work. As part of the research, a survey of social workers provided a view of the working conditions of social workers in 2009. About 49% of respondents worked more than their contracted hours; 9% worked over an additional nine hours a week; only 29% worked their contracted hours; 7% worked some time at the weekend and 35% worked at least one hour before 8.30am or after 7.30pm (Baginsky et al, 2009).

The nature of the type of work that social workers did was shown in their account of how their time was spent. Only 26% of their working time involved direct contact with clients, 34% on other case-related work in their agencies and 13% on inter-agency work, which constituted 73% of time with client-related work. 22% was spent recording case-related work. For those with electronic recording systems, they spent more time on recording case work than those social workers who did not use an electronic system (Baginsky et al, 2009).

Adequate supervision has been identified as essential for good quality social work. Two thirds of respondents reported that they received supervision every four weeks, with only 10% reporting that they received it more frequently. Some reported problems with prioritisation, sickness and vacancies that affected supervision. A quarter of frontline social workers in Children's Service Departments and over a third in Department of Adult Social Services were not receiving supervision every six weeks. One in four managers in Children's and Adult Social Services were also not receiving regular supervision. Although there was a general level of satisfaction with the quality of supervision received, many felt it was focused on case management, action planning and targets. Some respondents, especially more experienced social workers, regretted the lack of time to "reflect, develop, learn and unburden" (Baginsky et al, 2009) and the loss of collegiality.

The global financial crisis and austerity

The 2008/9 global financial crisis resulted in increased UK government intervention in the economy, through the partial nationalisation of two major banks. This was presented as an increased focus on the size of government debt. It could have been an opportunity to have a fundamental review of neo-liberalism and public management reforms (Engelen et al, 2012). This was reflected in a failure to acknowledge the impact of these policies.

Austerity policies introduced by the Conservative led coalition in 2010 were based on a deliberate misrepresentation of the UK's financial prospects. By 2018, the extent to which these policies are damaging public services through a reduction in resources is becoming clear, as is the extent of the attack on the role of the state in the provision of public services. The impact of austerity policies on a workforce which was already demoralised by the previous decades of public sector reforms is moving towards a crisis of public services, where regular questions about what it is possible to deliver are asked. There is also a growing public opinion that privatised utilities should be re-nationalised and the future of public services should be secured. These are reflected in current Labour Party policies. What is needed is a rethinking of how public services are delivered and the creation of a new model which brings together users and public professionals to preserve and extend services.

One of the major issues facing the future of public services is how to balance the delivery of a personalised service with services which are universal and are the product of a collective sense of responsibility. In trying to answer this question, the problem of how to meet individual needs within a universal and collective context can be helped by identifying how the individual contributes to the collective whole and similarly how the collective whole addresses individual needs. These relationships are particularly important in the delivery of community- based public services. This book proposes that the creation of more democratic processes would help to strengthen this relationship.

The need for public services to incorporate a stronger democratic element can be placed in the wider context of demands for political reform and a re-definition of the contract between citizens and government. Many countries are having to confront climate change and the impact of new technology on employment that require democratic interventions led by citizens and are informed by different levels of expertise instead of relying on a world dominated by large corporations and their profit-making business model.

Exploration of democratic professionalism

The following chapters will focus on the importance of democratic professionalism for the future of public service professionals and public services, using contemporary examples to illustrate what can be achieved with a more democratic approach, both individually and collectively. At this point in the ongoing crisis of public services, there are too few alternatives to draw on which present a future strategy for public services. After over forty years of privatisation and liberalisation, whether the private sector can deliver public services more efficiently or effectively than the public sector is still strongly contested and there is growing evidence to show that it has failed in several sectors. Indeed, the failure of privatisation in some services has resulted in a re-nationalisation process and a search for alternative ways of delivering public services.

This crisis for public service professionals and public services also has to be understood in terms of the impact of digitalisation, which is affecting the way in which public services are delivered and how professionals, whether in the public or private sectors, are viewed. Increased access to information on the Internet has led to a questioning of whether professionals are needed as a gateway to professional expertise and knowledge. There is also a wider criticism of experts and expert knowledge, which has its roots in the challenging of professional power.

One aim of this book is to both build on and challenge current practice in the education and training of public service professionals. A second will be to help policy makers and the public understand the key role that public service professionals play in the delivery of public services. The relationships that doctors, nurses, teachers and other public professionals create and maintain with service users are at the heart of effective public services. These are often ignored, and public service professionals are seen as the problem to be solved rather than as a resource to be nurtured. The predominance of women among public service professionals also affects how they are valued. There is extensive research to show that women are often not valued within organisations (Davies, 1996; Calás and Smircich, 1996; Wacjman, 1998; Calás and Smircich, 2006). In a similar way, people from Black and Minority Ethnic groups are often not valued and are underrepresented at higher levels of organisations, including public sector institutions (McGregor-Smith, 2017).

This book is for public service professionals, in training and in practice, who would like to have a more reflective sense of professional identity and a way of reviewing their relationships with clients, service users and students, so that they include a stronger sense of shared interests and democratic respect. The way in which the book offers new ideas and approaches to how to be a democratic professional is through an intellectual and practical journey to create a conceptual model which will encourage professionals to re-examine what their professional practice means. It will also challenge current assumptions about the relationship between public service professionals and service users, identifying the many different ways in which these two groups relate. From this exploration a more fundamental need emerges to re-define what collective and universal services are, and how they can be designed, delivered and evaluated by both service users and public professionals. The concept of democratic professionalism focuses on those delivering public services but links them to the service users who must be part of a coalition that takes control of the public sector.

Chapter 2 will develop a conceptual model of democratic professionalism which will facilitate the analysis of the three elements – expertise, respect/integrity and responsibility – and place the proposed action in a contemporary political context.

Some of the elements of democratic professionalism are already embodied in public institutions as a result of public management reforms but in a non-democratic way, for example, customer feedback. This book will then explore how democratic professionalism can be implemented in a more empowering way, both within existing public services and outside current institutional settings where public services are delivered (Chapters 3–5).

To make this book as practical as possible, a series of examples and case studies will illustrate the elements of democratic professionalism, from a group of public services which depend on the quality of interaction between services user and professional to be delivered successfully. They will include health care, social care, social services, education, planning and architecture. The examples have been chosen to illustrate the different nature of the service user: professional relationship. Examples have been chosen from a range of countries across the world. Although the main focus is the professional: user, there will also be examples which illustrate the relationship between professionals: communities and professionals: citizens.

2

A conceptual model of democratic professionalism

Although there is growing evidence to show that public services support economic and social development and contribute to greater social integration, there is currently a major challenge to the continuing existence of public services. Over the last thirty years of reforms there has been an increased use of the term 'professional' but it is used in the context of improving practice and does not reflect an increased sense of respect for professionals. This makes public services a difficult and challenging environment for public professionals who want to work towards change and a more democratic way of operating both for themselves and for service users. This chapter develops a conceptual model of democratic professionalism which will provide a strategy to show how professionals can operate more democratically and inform the future of democratic public services. The subsequent chapters will show how action can be taken, using examples from across the world.

As outlined in Chapter 1, the development of democratic professionalism can be seen as a reaction to public sector reforms, but is also a process of challenging the traditional notion of a professional and the exercise of professional power, which has often been undertaken by the public professionals themselves. The position of professionals in public services is part of a dynamic process shaped by the professions as well as by other interest groups. How this process can be facilitated in future will help to answer the question of how to enact democracy within public services that secure the future Welfare State.

Professionals and the state

The position of public service professionals is often presented as a contrast to that of a professional operating within a market and selling services, such as financial or accounting services. Legal services operate within public justice systems, but many lawyers often sell their services in a marketplace. Public service professionals are most often employed by the provider of services, which today may be public, for-profit or not-for-profit organisations.

Much sociological research on professionals analyses the functions and identity of professionals emphasising how professionals often work in groups which seek to exclude others. In contrast, by adopting a political analysis and trying to place public professionals within a political system, they can be seen as potentially having the capacity to take (political) action.

One way of understanding the nature of the relationship between public professionals and public services is to examine the relationship between public service professionals and the state. This is what defines public professionals as being different from professionals selling their services and operating in a market. T. H. Marshall, writing in 1939, highlighted politics as the unknown and unpredictable factor in the relationship between a public sector professional and the state, although he pointed out that the increasing technical nature of public services was shifting the balance of power away from politicians towards public sector professionals and administrators. This was before the creation of the Welfare State, although some of its foundations were already in place. It also raises the question of how public service professionals react when the state is changing. If public professionals have a role to play in initiating or participating in forms of political action, then this has to be considered in relation to different forms of professional agency.

Weber defined bureaucracy as the "monopolization of offices by academically trained experts with a distinctive status honour" (Collins, 1990: 16). The creation of a modern civil service was part of the process of separating "public monies and equipment" from private (domicile) (Weber, 1948: 197; see also 1914). The civil service official held office, which was seen as a form of vocation but required training, including examinations. The relationship between public officials was a more impersonal one than in business systems, which were dominated by personal relationships. The public official gained a more stable position which was not subject to personal influence and which often had the benefits of life tenure and a pension. The need for training led to officials being drawn from the most socially and economically privileged elites, who were most likely to have had access to training which gave them a technical expertise. However, the requirements for technical expertise led to changes and rationalisation in the systems of education and training.

Parsons (1939) developed a theory of professionalisation set in the context of bureaucratisation. He argued that professionals carried out their tasks with authority and autonomy. Professionals were motivated by altruism in providing services and maintaining standards rather than selling their labour or working for profit (Parsons, 1939). This was one of the early issues that distinguished public sector professionals from professionals operating within a market and selling their services.

In 1939, T. H. Marshall wrote about the changes experienced by professionals involved in providing services through a very early form of the Welfare State. He saw professionalism as "not concerned with self-interest, but with the welfare of the client" (Marshall, 1939: 332). There is "no need to abandon this individualism when the service is offered to a group or to a community" (Marshall, 1939: 332). He related the increased interest with the provision of social welfare that accompanied the evolution of a more democratic political system (Marshall, 1939: 333). With the introduction of the national health insurance scheme more services were made available to a larger part of society. The public professionals delivering these services were different from other more market-based professionals, because they worked for an employer as well as working for the community, although still saw people as individuals. It is this dual perspective of working with individuals as well as providing a public/community service which characterises public professionals. This supports the position of professionals operating within the Welfare State.

Durkheim (1958) discussed the role of professional groups, particularly medical and legal professionals, as mediators between the state and the individual. In this sense, he contributed to a structural analysis of professions. Durkheim argued that professional associations could contribute to political structures and representation (Durkheim, 1958: 99, 104). This was partly based on observations that the links and sense of shared values that bring people in the same occupational group together are often stronger than their sense of regional or geographical identity. However, Durkheim's ethical sense of occupation has implications for the potential role of professionals and their associations in government and in society, because the ties of the professional association may be in conflict with clients or government.

Scott (2008) proposed an "institutional conception of professions" which drew from earlier work on the study of institutions. He argued for professions as institutional agents but not as a homogenous group. Instead, he defined three categories. First, 'creative' professionals, whose role is to expand and justify aspects of professionalism. Second, 'carrier' professionals, which includes groups such as teachers, consultants, lawyers and librarians, who 'carry' professional messages to their clients and the public. Third, 'clinical' professionals, such as scientists, engineers and accountants who "apply professional solutions to specific problems, whether individual clients, corporations or public agencies" (Scott, 2008: 228). The importance of this view is that it provides a way of explaining the differences between professionals and how they operate.

Scott (2008) wrote about the institutional analysis of organisations and acknowledged that "cultural cognitive frameworks" can "provide the deeper foundations of institutional forms" (Scott, 2008: 429). Rules, norms and meanings arise in interaction, and they are preserved and modified by the behaviour of social actors (Giddens, 1979). DiMaggio looked at the role of agency and conflict among different officers in art museums in the US (1991) "as professional factions competed for control". He linked institutional theory to Giddens' structuration theory (1979), which brought together structural arguments with theories of agency: "structures being both the product of and a context for action" (Scott, 2008: 438).

Structuration theory discussed how professional groups can deal with a changing institutional environment. It deals both with individual agency and the reproduction of institutional structures. Professionals have to balance both agency and structure in their working lives. Structuration theory is based on a belief that social activities are "continually recreated by social actors via the means whereby they express themselves as actors" (Giddens, 1984: 2).

Giddens explained structures as processes which are constantly produced and reproduced. Structural properties are defined as rules and resources and structure allows practices to operate over time and space. Structuration theory argued that rules and resources, which are drawn upon in the production and reproduction of social action are, at the same time, the means of system reproduction (Giddens, 1984: 19). Agents and structures are seen as part of a duality, rather than as independent concepts (Hardcastle et al, 2005). This is useful in understanding how public service professionals can develop any form of action.

Public professionals and the changing role of state

Perhaps the most fundamental question facing a public service professional in the early 21st century is how to define their relationship with the state in a period when the role and structure of the state is changing, moving from the welfare state, to the contractual and market state to what has been defined as the Consolidation State (Streek, 2016).

In 1939, T. H. Marshall published an article on the newly emerging group of professionals who were working to implement social policies in municipalities, charities and social welfare agencies. These new professionals were employed by the public sector or voluntary organisations in contrast to traditional professionals who sold their services to the public. He observed that the services which these new groups were starting to deliver were essentially non-standardised. *"It is unique and personal"*, something which is common to all skilled labour. The way in which the public service professionals operate brings their own personality and personal beliefs into their work. These qualities cannot be measured and are given in service to the public.

A second issue that T. H. Marshall discussed in relation to these public professionals is the sense of duty to both the individual and the community and the interests of society. Although governments (or professional associations) may issue public policies and legislation that will dictate or influence the action of a public professional, the way in which professionals delivering public services make decisions is still dependent on their own professional judgements. However, the way in which public professionals balance their duty to the community has been uneven, with professional disciplines which take a more collective/holistic approach, for example, public health, town planning, not receiving the same status as those which concentrate on services delivered directly to the individual.

T. H. Marshall did not see a potential conflict between the professional providing a service to an individual and "the principles of political obligations" (Marshall, 1939: 334). He saw that the quality of the service depended on the relationship between the public professional and the client (Marshall, 1939: 331) and politics played a key role in the work of public sector professionals (Marshall, 1939: 334). The "authority exercised by the social services... rests not only on the superior knowledge of the administrators but also on the political power derived from the constitution". He argued that the welfare of the client benefits from the individual nature of the service delivery but this must also be seen in social terms. "There is nothing in this attitude which is fundamentally antagonistic to public services or social planning" (Marshall, 1939: 332). However, due to the increased technical complexity of public services the balance of power was moving from the politician to the administrator (Marshall, 1939: 335). He saw public professionals as being socialised and public services as being professionalised (Marshall, 1939: 335). He quoted Sir Kaye Le Fleming, speaking at the BMA meeting in 1938:

> You will remember that you have duties to the profession as a whole, to the public as a whole, and to the State. (Marshall, 1939: 336)

Even in the pre-Welfare State period, there was increased team work which brought different types of professionals together within public services and contributed to a changing sense of professional identity. It also highlighted some of the difficulties that professionals faced in taking the interests of the community as the heart of their professionalism.

By 1950, the Welfare State in the UK had become more tangible in that health services, social services and education had become established as universal public services, free at the point of access, delivered by public service professionals. In reflecting the changes since 1939, when Marshall first started to identify public sector professionals as separate and different to other professionals, he conceptualised the term 'social citizenship' to encompass what public sector professionals were responsible for implementing. The challenge to public sector professionals in the early days of the Welfare State was to recognise the importance of professionals understanding that individual goals must be balanced with wider collective ideals.

The concept of 'civic professionalism' provided a way of linking 'public service professionals' to the social rights of citizenship, which were central to the establishment of new systems of social welfare after the Second World War. Marshall (1950) emphasised altruism or the 'service' orientation of professionalism. He identified civil, political and social rights as three components of citizenship. Social rights covered access to health, education and welfare and complemented civil and political rights. Marshall argued that 'public service professionals' played an integral role in ensuring that these rights were recognised, which may require some form of action to support the citizen's access to public services.

There has been some questioning of Marshall's concept of citizenship rights, because the state may work in the interest of more than one group but to the exclusion of others. This is particularly relevant in relation to the development of the Welfare State where the goal of universality may lead to a denial of difference and diversity (Lawy and Biesta, 2006). It has implications for the roles that 'public service professionals' play in public service delivery and the extent to which they challenged discrimination and oppression.

In understanding the way in which public professionals can take action, it is important to recognise that the term "Welfare State" covers a wide range of different arrangements, even though the aims of providing public services and social welfare using principles of shared risk and universal services may be similar. Arts and Gelissen (2002) characterised different welfare systems according to de-commodification, which looks at the extent that services are given as a matter of right and whether a welfare system strengthens social solidarity.

Mackintosh (1996) argued that welfare systems are the result of social settlements which attempt to bridge class divides in societies. However, the state is not the equal arbiter that it presents itself as, being "a moment of the class struggle that seeks to regulate the class struggle" (Neary, 1997: 12). In this context, social policies provide incentives and disincentives that encourage or discourage individuals and groups to follow a particular path of policy development (Esping-Andersen, 1990).

The publication of 'In and Against the State' (1979) was one of the most important contributions to the process of professionals questioning the ways of working within the state and how they could change and improve the way in which public services were delivered. It articulated some of the contradictions in working for the state.

> As workers in those occupations that are termed 'professional', such as social work, or teaching, we are often given impossible problems to solve arising from poverty or from the powerlessness of our 'clients'. (London Edinburgh Weekend Return Group, 1980: Chapter 1)

Its publication in 1979 and 1980 was an indication of how the 1970s had generated a growing interest in developing ways of improving the practice and delivery of public services, particularly in relation to more democratic relations with service users. Another perspective, which the book provided, can be related to compromises involved in working within a bureaucracy which made professionals want to improve their practice whilst trying to address some of the structural issues facing their clients. The publication of 'In and Against the State' was an attempt to make some recommendations about how to act within such a conflicting environment.

Writing in 1990, at a time when questioning of the long-term viability of the Welfare State had started, Bertilson stated that the Welfare State is anchored in "the strength of its professional ventures" (Bertilson, 1990: 124). Professionals are an integral part of the modern state (Freidman, 2001). The social rights of individual citizens are reproduced by professionals as part of their professional practice. This can initially be interpreted as professionals playing a benign role in guaranteeing the social rights of citizens but it can also become more controlling. Professionals play a role in the process of governmentality and in keeping the population in control. "Social service professionals" play a role in policy implementation and often determine the nature and extent of implementation. In this sense, they have been seen as agents of policy (Damaska, 1986).

Esping-Andersen questioned whether the "Welfare State" is a sum of national social policies or whether it is an institutional force in its own right (Esping-Andersen, 1990; Arts and Gelissen, 2002), which has implications for the public professionals operating within it. One approach to understanding the "Welfare State" has been to examine the similarities and differences between different national systems of social welfare in order to develop typologies of social welfare. Esping-Andersen (1990, 1999) identified three ideal-types: conservative, liberal and social democratic systems, each one reflecting different arrangements made between the state, market and family. Esping-Andersen located the United Kingdom as part of the liberal system, along with the United States, Canada and Australia, in which means-tested assistance and limited universal services were targeted at working class groups. This was in contrast with the Nordic region, which Esping-Andersen characterised as a social democratic system, with higher levels of equality within society, including middle-class participation in universal benefits.

There has been extensive debate stimulated by the Esping-Andersen model, although he has admitted that there are overlaps between all three models. It is based on an analysis of the system of welfare benefits and eligibility based on employment, rather than the role that professionals played within these systems. There are some common characteristics between the UK and the social democratic model, because middle-class groups have participated in many of the benefits of the Welfare State, especially in health and education, but not equally, because the educated middle class were given a role, which "reinforced the notion that the middle-class was a distinct social group entitled to special treatment" (Todd, 2014: 168).

This position is further supported by the work of Bertilson (1990) who argued that professionals play different roles in the Liberal and Welfare States. In the Liberal State, professionals operate within a market, both regulating and being regulated. In the Welfare State, the law plays a pivotal role, with professionals regulated and being regulated by the law (Bertilson, 1990: 115). Another difference between these two types of state occurs regarding the position of citizens. In the Liberal State, citizens have civil rights but in the Welfare State, citizens have a much wider range of social rights. Professions work in a professional-client relationship within the Liberal State but in the Welfare State, the relationship becomes more complex with the professions working in state bureaucracies and delivering services shaped by this bureaucratic setting (Bertilson, 1990: 118). Professionals play an important role in guaranteeing social rights for citizens in the Welfare State, which is a political act as well as a professional one.

In countries where the welfare system is organised on a more local basis, for example, Finland, professionals have not necessarily become such an integral part of the public sector and so professional projects were not linked to the public sector (Henriksson, et al, 2006). However, in England, the post-1945 social reforms and the establishment of the Welfare State saw a gradual involvement of central government in the professional development of some public services professionals, for example, teachers and social workers, although local government was responsible for the delivery of services. This centralised role of central government has increased with public management reforms.

The role of public service professionals in the provision of universal services can be framed as part of citizenship. Wrede (2008) drew on Gramsci's concept of cultural 'hegemony' (Gramsci, 1971) and the role of organic intellectuals, who are defined as intellectuals who promote the interests of a specific class, rather than traditional intellectuals who were supposed to speak over and above the interests of a particular class. In Finland, 'social services professionals' campaigned for the creation of a Welfare State and increased democratisation within healthcare. Social rights were instituted in the Welfare State, particularly in primary health care. The previously professionally dominated health care system was replaced by a new bureaucracy with health care professionals as employees.

The nature of 'public service professionals' began to change with the questioning and reforms of the Welfare State. The introduction of teaching assistants, nursing and healthcare assistants and other roles that support professionals can be seen as new types of 'public service professional'. The resulting changed relationship between professions and the Welfare State has been further analysed and described as "the rise of a 'new' professionalism", which is more accountable to the changing needs of the population (Kuhlmann and Saks, 2008: 55).

Public sector reforms

The introduction of public sector reforms oversaw the transformation of public sector institutions and this has had an impact on 'public service professionals' because the Welfare State underwent structural changes as part of this process. Although the overall change to the state after 1979 can be described as the introduction of the 'contractual' state, the functional changes to the state in the period from 1979 to 2015 have been characterised as moving through three stages (see Table 2).

The transformation of the state continues. The stages outlined above attempt to chart the pattern of change since the 1980s.

Table 2: Changes in the role of the state 1980–2010s

Period	From	To
1980-1990s	Hollowed-out state	Regulatory state
2000s	Market/contractual/"congested"	
2010s	Lean/mean state	Consolidation state

Sources: Rhodes, 1994; Sketcher 2000, Rhodes, 2007; Streek, 2016

They will be discussed below, using examples to illustrate how the changing nature of the state changed the Welfare State, the delivery of public services and consequently the role of public service professionals.

The transformation of the state started with the civil services contracting out delivery of services to quangos. By 1983, compulsory competitive tendering (CCT) was introduced, which required both local authorities and the NHS to put ancillary services, such as catering, cleaning and facilities management, out to tender. The private sector was considered able to provide these services more cheaply than the public sector, although the reduction in costs was achieved by reducing wages. Contracting out of services was accompanied by a change in language where citizens or service users became customers or consumers. For public services to be bought and sold, the way in which they were described had to change from being represented in a holistic view of a service to the division of a service into a series of tasks, making it possible for these tasks to be bought and sold. This process is known as commodification (Leys, 2001; Rhodes, 2007). This is accompanied by the transformation of citizens to consumers. The introduction of consumerism to public services affected the relationship between service providers and service users or consumers by introducing a new set of values, reflecting a more business-focused approach to delivery. In schools and colleges, after 1988, schools managed their own budgets and parents were expected to make their choice of schools using performance indicators (Jones, 2002). Universities are currently trying to assess the impact of students becoming consumers on the culture and values of teaching and learning (Naidoo, 2008).

These changes introduced a new way of operating for the state, which changed from being a public service provider to a commissioner of services (Osborne and Gaebler, 1992; King, 2007). This process led to the conceptualisation of the State as a "hollowed out" or managerial state (Rhodes, 1994). More specifically, it was seen to be "hollowed out" from above, by the EU, from within through a process of marketisation and sideways through Next Steps agencies (Sketcher, 2000). These changes also led to public policies being created for and with a stronger private sector influence (Rhodes, 1994; Rhodes, 1997).

In 1990, the NHS and local authorities were reorganised into internal markets with commissioners responsible for commissioning and contracting services and providers, either within the public sector or the not-for-profit and for-profit service providers. This increased the commodification of public services no longer seen as part of democratic citizenship but becoming increasingly commercialised (Leys, 2001). In order to function as a quasi-market, public sector institutions were subject to corporatisation and had to operate within business objectives, aiming to make a profit, working to targets and new quality standards. With the introduction of commissioning and contracting, the state had to take on new roles. In order to secure the quality of public services which were not being delivered by the state, quality standards, new regulatory agencies and regular inspections were introduced (Neave, 1998; Hood et al, 1999; Moran, 2004; King, 2006; King, 2007). What had started as a "hollowing out" of the state, with the state no longer the sole provider of public services, evolved into the state taking on a "regulatory" and "evaluative" role, almost replacing its role as service provider. The responsibility for delivery is contracted out while power contracts to the centre.

The concept of the regulatory state has its origins in the United States with the development of rule-making, bureaucratic processes of the administrative state and is associated with the expansion of outsourcing and privatisation (Levi-Faur, 2013). Majone (2010) considered the main function of the regulatory state to be to correct market failures. The regulatory functions of government are separated from policy making as the regulatory agencies are outside government. Accountability is taken away from government and assigned to less democratic institutions. Levi-Faur (2013) defined the regulatory state as a state that applies and extends rule-making, monitoring and enforcement via bureaucratic organs of the state (Hood et al, 1999; Levi-Faur, 2013).

The implementation of the Education Reform Act (1988) illustrates how the form of the state changed during this period (Ainley, 2001). The introduction of a National Curriculum, which each state-run school had to teach, was accompanied by the creation of regulatory agencies to inspect each school to see that it was adhering to the national curriculum and related quality standards. The results of these inspections were published as a series of league tables, thus introducing an element of competition between schools. The creation of an audit culture and different ways of measuring performance were introduced throughout the public sector (Neave, 1998; Moran, 2004). For public professionals, these reforms led to their decisions being questioned by a strong prevailing managerial culture.

There was a continuity in the policies pursued by the New Labour government after 1979 with the previous 18 years of Tory administration. The New Labour government adopted many of the public reform ideas of the previous Conservative government, aiming to develop a fundamental partnership between labour and business. New ways of working between public and private sectors had been introduced in 1992, with the creation of public–private partnerships as a way of leveraging new sources of capital to invest in improvements to public infrastructure, and these continued to be encouraged after 1997 (Gaffney et al, 1999; Hellowell and Pollock 2007). Both commissioners and providers of services were encouraged to form networks, which linked a range of public and private players together in terms of shared interests or common service provision. These introduced new forms of governance which sometimes struggled to meet the needs of all stakeholders, with service-users often left unrecognised. Ultimately, networks led to greater complexity, as seen in new bureaucracies and in the relations of the state with a range of providers (Sketcher, 2000).

By the 2000s "collaborative institutions had become a core resource in all areas of UK public policy. This rich web of linkages arose in response to the problems inherent in the fragmentation arising from hollowing-out" (Sketcher, 2000: 3). The following decade saw some significant changes in the way in which both the public, for-profit and not-for-profit sectors worked together. The nature of the state in this period of growing relational complexity has been called the 'congested' or entrepreneurial state (Mazzucatto, 2011). Towards the end of the 2000s, there was a more consistent questioning of the effectiveness of regulation and inspection, showing that effective regulation in a market had not been achieved. By 2018, the nature of the state could be described as more "hollowed out" than congested and the process of contracting out of public services had moved on to out-sourcing and more privatisation (Rhodes, 1994; Sketcher, 2000; Rhodes, 2007). The private sector continued to consolidate its position in the public policy process and has become a dominant influence in many government departments (Player and Leys, 2010).

The concept of the Consolidation State (Streeck, 2016) has been developed to explain some of the changes that have taken place since 2008 and the global financial crisis, which had an impact on many states because governments had to nationalise the financial sector, a reassertion of the role of the state in the economy. The indebtedness of states had increased since the 1980s, with some stabilisation after the 1990s, but continued after 2008. One factor contributing to greater indebtedness was the decline in tax revenues, a result of countries competing to reduce taxes for corporations and high-income earners (Streeck, 2016: 116). The increase in borrowing was also related to globalisation and the process of financialisation, which enabled borrowing through a wider range of products and instruments. This helped governments to access more credit and so postpone making decisions to reduce their indebtedness.

A response to crisis

Financial services became one of the fastest growing sectors. However, the global financial crisis of 2008 made the position of indebted governments unsustainable. Financial markets wanted to be assured that governments had their long-term debt under control. Austerity policies were introduced by many governments as a way of reducing public expenditure, with the aim of reducing the size of the state (Streek, 2016). Institutional restructuring abandoned democratic principles because of concerns about the confidentiality of commercial interests.

This new phase in the changing role of the state has serious implications for public services and public professionals. Already affected by several decades of public sector reforms, the continued under-investment in public services and the imposition of targets and league tables, public service professionals have been affected directly by the outsourcing and privatisation of public services. There are implications for public professionals in terms of what action they can take in relation to service users. The increased commodification of public services has changed the way in which the work of the public sector professional is perceived, the nature of their labour and the way in which their working days are organised. Many have lost control over their labour process. The labour element of public services is even less valued and is often provided by a fragmented workforce. Public professionals are regularly challenged in their professional decisions. For many public professionals the possibility of taking action to make public services more democratic in design, delivery and governance may seem remote.

Hannah Arendt's *vita activa*

In order to develop a strategy to make public services more democratic, this book will now draw on Hannah Arendt's '*vita activa*' as outlined in *The Human Condition* (1958). Published in 1958 during a period of rapid technological and social change, *The Human Condition* aimed to "reconsider the human condition from the newest experiences and most recent fears" and "to think about what we are doing" (Arendt, 1958: 5). Arendt, informed by a critique of mass consumer society, explored the concept of the *vita activa*, which has three components: labour, work and action. 'Labour' is the biological process of the human body, which is needed to survive/reproduce/continue; 'work' is the activity which creates objects and 'action' which through speech and action and is the condition for all political life (Arendt, 1958: 7).

She provides a framework that can start to explore how to take action towards becoming a democratic professional. Kreber (2015), Biesta (2007/10), Papadimos (2009) and Ranson (2018) have all used Arendt's *vita activa* in relation to democratic professionalism in education, medicine and nursing. This book argues that the *vita activa* has a wider application to many more professionals delivering public services, and the concept of the *vita activa* can contribute to a better understanding of how public services could function.

Arendt saw action as the exclusive prerogative of human beings, who bring action together with being. They recognise the value of political activity and the capacity to change the world through action. A basic question which informs the analysis is whether people are social or political animals. The dominance of consumerism and the future of democratic action have many parallels in an analysis of contemporary society in the early 21st century. There are two aspects of Arendt's *vita activa* which are relevant for identifying new ways of working towards democratic professionalism. The components of the *vita activa* can be used as a way of analysing the work of public professionals and the means that Arendt identifies as necessary to take action – plurality, the public sphere and natality – provide a framework for democratic professionals taking action.

Arendt saw the functioning of Greek civic society as a way of explaining the role of the *vita activa* to understand the nature of democratic action as well as the nature of labour and work. In terms of how this will be used to provide a conceptual model for democratic professionalism, it is useful to draw on feminist criticism of Arendt. This has been extensive because of her gender-blind approach, which portrayed the role of women in Greek civil society as responsible for reproducing the household and hence having a limited role in political action (Dietz, 1991; Kopola, 1997). Yet, women form the majority of public service professionals and any analysis of how public service professionals can take action has to include a gendered perspective. Dietz (1991) argued that Arendt's *vita activa* and her concepts of action and plurality could inform a feminist theory of politics. The importance of *The Human Condition* is that it provides an opportunity for reflection on how to take collective action (Dietz, 1991: 248). The importance of taking action in the public realm, which creates a sense of solidarity between the individuals involved, should be at the core of women's actions and those of Black and Minority Ethnic groups within the public sector.

This book adopts this approach of using the three elements of the *vita activa* in relation to public services. It is not a literal interpretation of the three types of the *vita activa* but it uses them as a way to examine relationships and the potential for action in public services today. It will also address the question of how women and Black and Minority Ethnic public professionals can take action.

Labour

Labour and work form two elements of the *vita activa*. Arendt pointed out that although many European languages have two words for labour and work, there has been little written about their differences in either political theories or theories of labour (Arendt, 1958: 80). Labouring has traditionally not been valued. Arendt draws on Greek civic society, where the '*polis*' was for men who did not have to labour. Those who had to labour did it because of the need to meet their daily needs. Work was valued more because it created objects, some of which were for use but others became commodities for exchange, eventually contributing to the development of a consumer society. This separation between labour and work is reflected in the contemporary distinctions between skilled/unskilled work and manual/intellectual labour, which provoke unresolved debates about how to value what is sometimes called unproductive labour, unskilled labour or manual labour. Guy Standing (2011, 2014) has discussed the importance of recognising the difference between labour and work, using care as a type of labour which is not valued.

Considering the work of public service professionals in this context of labour and work can reveal some of the less tangible aspects of how they deliver public services. Much of the work of public service professionals is often not recognised or valued. For example, many public services include some dimension of caring, whether nursing, social care, social work or education. This can be seen as what Arendt described as 'labouring', a repetitive activity which is necessary for survival of the client but is often monotonous.

This view of care as a form of labouring can be supported by recent research (Gill et al, 2017) which looked at the relationships between policy and care, which are conventionally seen as different activities. When examined more carefully, policy is seen as a 'set of open-ended practices; policy is performed and re-performed in particular sites and settings and by particular actors and … a kind of ongoing and distributed "doing"'. There are contradictions in many public policies which are seen as resulting in a lack of care. Bringing care and policy together provides a way of examining care within a political context. Rather than care being something that is done to someone, it allows for a different and more nuanced understanding of care. Singleton and Mee (2017) call for "an appreciation of the specific and situated ways in which care is done, figuring care as a selective, affectively charged mode of attention" (Gill et al, 2017: 14).

Work

In contrast, there are many (in)tangible parts of public services which have parallels with a creative form of work, for example medicine, teaching, social work, higher education. The creativity comes from the processes of diagnosis, application of knowledge, imagination and communication with one or more service users. Although not creating a tangible product, the public service user may leave the consultation or interaction in a changed state to when they entered the service or they know that they have access to treatment, teaching or another type of intervention which will change them. In this sense, the delivery of public services is a transformational process in which public service professionals and service users are both involved. It can also be seen as a starting point for a more focused and democratic relationship between public professional and service user. The encouragement of patients to self-manage their conditions is a form of democratic sharing of knowledge drawing from the patient's interpretation of their own experience and using this knowledge to inform a way of managing their condition. With an increase in limiting long-term conditions, this is an important development.

For the public service professional, this combination of delivering a transformational service underpinned by an unrecognised type of labouring has been made more complicated by public sector reforms because the imposition of targets, assessments and league tables has changed what had been a transformational service into a more routine and controlled process. Both the 'labouring' and 'work' aspects of public services have been subject to commodification in order for public services to be costed and commissioned but this results in a fragmented service, which is unsatisfactory from both the service user's and the public professional's perspective.

Plurality, natality and the public sphere

Plurality

It is not just the elements of the *vita activa* which can be applied to public professionals and public services. Arendt emphasized three beliefs that underpin any democratic action: plurality; the public sphere and natality. It is these three beliefs which can contribute to an appreciation of how to take action and move towards different forms of democratic professionalism. Human plurality is a basic condition for both action and speech and, Arendt argued, brings equality and distinctiveness together. She wrote:

> If (wo)men were not equal, they could neither understand each other and those who came before them, nor plan for the future and foresee the needs of those who will come after them. (Arendt, 1958: 175)

She saw equality as central to understanding the past and present as well as informing the view of the future. But people are also distinct from each other. Speech and action reveal this distinctiveness and contribute to how we place ourselves in the world (p.176).

> Speech corresponds to the fact of distinctness and is the actualisation of the human condition of plurality, that is, of living as a distinct and unique being among equals. (Arendt, 1958: 178)

Speech and action contribute to people revealing themselves in a setting where people are gathered together but are not necessarily polarised into different (political) positions (Arendt, 1958: 179). Action and speech retain the capacity for people to reveal themselves even if talking about objective matters. Action and speaking do not create tangible results or products because they are part of the *"fabric of human relationships and affairs"* (Arendt,1958:95) which depend on human plurality. However, action is not possible in isolation because it affects others, establishes relationships and cuts across boundaries (Arendt, 1958: 190). Its scope is extensive and unpredictable. The political realm rises directly out of acting together through the sharing of words and deeds.

Kreber (2014) and Biesta (2012) use Arendt's analysis as a framework for professional life which includes taking action as well as emphasizing plurality, a world where the multiple views of members are valued and shared as equals and freedom is connected to others (Biesta, 2012). The potential of this view can be seen in a society that has increasing inequalities and a strong, consumer-led individualism. Arendt was writing in the 1950s, at a time when the term mass consumerism was used to describe changes in society, characterised by a more intense form of individualism. This is also the case in the early 21st century, where individualism is actively promoted and acknowledged in society as a whole and in public services, which previously had been considered as universal, shared services. An issue which links these two time periods is the impact of increased individualism on democratic processes and social development. Arguing for action in public services is part of a process of addressing the tensions between the individual and collective interest but a belief in plurality is a way of reconciling these tensions.

Public sphere

Arendt highlighted the separation of the private and public spheres and its relation to action. She showed how the concepts of public and private realms evolved, which can help to show the dynamics of the public realm and public services. Drawing from the Greek experience of the 'polis' when the household and its economic activities became linked to the public realm, which resulted in housekeeping and family issues becoming a collective concern, she shows how the private and public realms merged into each other (Arendt, 1958: 30). Again, this is one interpretation of *The Human Condition* that has been controversial. Taking a literal interpretation of the separation of the public and private spheres makes it difficult to apply to the delivery of public services. However, a more subtle interpretation about how public and private spheres interact and overlap provides a more useful framework for examining how public services are expected to transcend the public and the private, depending on where they are delivered. For example, the delivery of home care is a public service delivered in a domestic/private sphere which has particular challenges for both the home care worker, who is entering a private sphere, and the service user, who is receiving a public service in their home. It is also at the core of some of the dilemmas facing public services, which are trying to deliver public services in personalised forms yet within the context of a universal service and collective responsibility.

What role do public professionals play in shaping the public realm? Arendt argued that the creation of a public realm or public space required a long-term perspective and a sense of permanence, which a consumer society lacks. She thought that "we have lost the capacity for speech and action since the social realm has banished them to private and intimate spheres" (p.49). A public realm can gather people together and create a community but mass society has lost the "power to gather people together". Ranson (2018) sees Arendt's importance as capturing "the distinctiveness of agency in the public sphere and to rescue it from those notions of action... driven by necessities of consumption... rather than expressions of freedom which characterises action in the public sphere" (Ranson, 2018: 57).

In these interpretations, the continuity of public services and the place of public professionals in delivering them can provide a sense of continuity in a rapidly changing society. There are many cases where this has happened in the past, for example, the role of the general practitioner or the way in which a local school has remained a stable element in a community. This will become increasingly important in a society as a result of digitisation and the dismantling of the Welfare State.

Natality

Natality and the sense of starting something new is an essential step in taking action. There are several ways to interpret natality. The most immediate one is that natality means being born. It is a new beginning and so, by being born, human beings are capable of action (Arendt, 1958: 8-9). Arendt argued that human beings are unique in being able to act and make new beginnings. This uniqueness is grounded in the capacity for speech and action. Another interpretation is that human birth stimulates the creation of inter-personal relationships, which is another type of action, because a child must act, establish a place in the world and this forces others to act (Totschnig, 2017: 344). This type of action is more linked to creating a place in the world in relation to other people, which has an overtly political dimension. Wolfhart Totschnig (2017) makes the connection between natality and politics in "natality as the constant arrival of newcomers underlies the continuing existence of the realm of politics" (Totschnig, 2017: 344).

Taking action

The concepts of labour, work and action in the *vita activa* are applicable to the position of public service professionals because they help to reveal the nature of the relationship between how public services are delivered and how public professionals can start to identify future political action with service users (Figure 1). It acknowledges that the delivery of public services encompasses several activities, not just the mechanical delivery of a service, but contributes to a democratic process in which public professionals support and work in partnership with citizens as part of the process of designing, planning, delivering and evaluating public services.

Arendt showed how action has to be informed by a belief in the importance of plurality, the public sphere and natality. It is interesting to compare these three beliefs to Dewey's

Figure 1: Public services and the *vita activa*

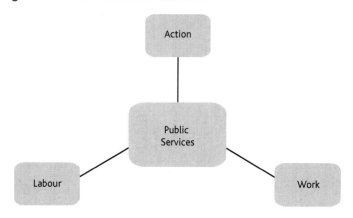

three principles for democratic institutions and the underlying principles of democratic professionalism outlined by Taubman (2011) in Chapter 1. Table 3 shows that there are considerable overlaps between the three principles.

Arendt presented the case for taking action within a society that was focused on mass consumerism. She thought that people are essentially political beings who need to take opportunities to develop a public realm which will facilitate

Table 3: Comparison of Dewey, Arendt and Taubman principles for democratic action

Dewey (1916, 1939)	Arendt (1958)	Taubman (2011)
Access to information to inform democratic decisions and action	Plurality – world where the multiple views of members are valued and shared as equals and freedom is connected to others	Facilitate access to ideas and information and critical reflection and evaluation;
Helping to balance individual and shared interests	Public/private spheres	Believe in the capacity of people (individual and collective);
How people deal with each other (attitude of human beings)	Belief in natality to take action	Have a concern for others, "the common good", for their dignity and rights

Source: Dewey, 1916, 1939; Arendt, 1958; Taubman, 2011

political action. Democratic professionals can take on this role but this requires a better understanding of how they can address the three underlying principles of taking action (Arendt) or establishing democracy within institutions and society (Dewey and Taubman).

The emergence of democratic professionalism as a reaction to the imposition of a Consolidation State by public service professionals has placed them in the position of trying to identify and establish settings in which democratic professionalism can be exercised. Current discussions about democracy in public services and how to create more democratic spaces are part of this process. It may involve how to change current economic policies or it may be how to provide support to communities in struggles for resources and services or working to identify and define new ways of addressing social and economic problems. The following three chapters set out how democratic professionals can start to take action by using these three basic principles:

Chapter 3: identifying diverse sources of expertise (plurality);
Chapter 4: developing an inclusive public sphere;
Chapter 5: having a belief in the capacity to act.

3

Identifying diverse sources of expertise

This chapter argues that the challenge that faces public professionals operating as democratic professionals is to respect other sources of expertise as well as to understand how they are constituted and how to facilitate their use. The definition of expertise which will be used in this book is that the combination of knowledge and skills creates expertise. This is generated through practical experience combined with theoretical study and learning (Polanyi, 1958; Polanyi, 1966).

Crouch (2015) showed how the market over-simplifies the knowledge needed to run public services, undermines professional expertise and leads to short term 'gaming' of the system. The fragmentation of public services has damaged the quality and destroyed much institutional knowledge which is handed down and exchanged between public professionals (Whitty, 2000: Ball, 2008). The relationship of the democratic professional to the building up of expertise will have to change and the recognition of the value of diverse sources of expertise will necessarily change perceptions of what constitutes professional knowledge and expertise. At the same time as acknowledging the diverse sources of knowledge and expertise, the democratic professional will have to engage with the tensions and conflicts arising from a widespread distrust of experts and expert knowledge.

Knowledge, skills and expertise

Drawing the concept of 'human plurality' from Hannah Arendt's *vita activa*, which she defined as a "basic condition of both action and speech, has the twofold character of equality and distinction"

(Arendt, 1958: 175) informs an analysis of how knowledge and skills contribute to different ways of seeing the world and to understanding different worlds (Arendt, 1958; Ranson, 2018). It can help to appreciate different life-worlds and so inform the creation of the public sphere. For a democratic professional wanting to examine knowledge, skills and expertise within public services from a democratic perspective, acknowledging plurality will have to inform an analysis of the types of knowledge and skills that underpin existing public services as well as the impact that outsourcing and privatisation have had on the knowledge and skills base used to run public services.

Traditionally the role of professionals has been to act as guardians of privileged expertise. Democratic professionalism provides expert opinions in more accessible ways, but this does not mean that experts are redundant; rather they have to operate with more diverse and pluralist sources of knowledge and information. Some of the reasons for the current hostility to expert opinions will now be discussed.

As well as the deliberately distorting effects of anti-social media, there is a growing questioning of the value of professional expert knowledge because of cases where the professional judgement of a public professional was found to be incorrect or lacking in rigour, resulting in damage to a patient or client. In the United Kingdom, the case of the GP Harold Shipman, the death of Baby P and other cases where professionals either did harm intentionally or where professionals failed to protect a child or patient have made people question the value of professionals. This is especially in relation to the provision of healthcare, social work and other services which require a specialist assessment of risk and care.

This challenging of professionals is not new, but the increasing use of human rights and equal opportunities frameworks and legislation make the rights of individuals recognised in a way that they were not in the past. Democratic professionals must respond and acknowledge that mistakes and poor judgements were made in the past and try to develop ways of working which incorporate a wider source of knowledge and expertise, informed by service users. Public ignorance and superstition often make this difficult.

Democratic public services would need to draw from a diverse approach to sources of knowledge, recognise a wider range of skills and so define a multi-faceted, democratic type of expertise. Before trying to create a democratic expertise, it is helpful to try to understand the origins of the words, 'expert' and 'expertise'. Raymond Williams (1976), an expert who tried to put his knowledge to public use, found that the origin of the word 'expert' was *expertus* which means 'to try' or 'do' and that 'experts' emerged in the nineteenth century as part of industrialisation, which placed an emphasis on specialisation and qualifications. The terms 'layperson' or 'one of the people' were seen as the opposite of expert (Williams, 1976), thus obscuring the value of a wide range of different sources of knowledge and skills, gained through experience. The interpretation of expert as someone who 'tries' and 'does' goes beyond being able to do and complete a task competently and helps to inform the delivery of public services. However, it also contributes to a polarising process which devalues many sources of expertise, including those of services users and local communities.

Since the 1960s, the concept of 'expertise' has been used more frequently (Eyal, 2013: 869) and this coincides with a greater questioning of professional power and the rise of social and user movements which campaigned for greater participation in the design and delivery of public services. This has resulted in the development of alliances and coalitions between service users, families and professionals which have all contributed to the development of expertise around a condition or disability, for example, members of the Mental Patients Union were supported by doctors and other health workers. The aim of these movements has been to make the expertise of services users obtained through experience valued as much as expertise gained through study. Health professionals do not experience these conditions directly. Eyal (2013) argued that instead of thinking in terms of a sociology of professionals, a sociology of expertise is more relevant for trying to identify which knowledge and skills are most significant.

Cambrosio et al (1992) examined expertise as "the central theme of enquiry...to reconstruct links between scientific activity and what traditional approaches used to call 'the wider social context'" (Cambrosio et al, 1992: 342). They viewed the term 'expert' as a term which has not just come out of scientific practice but has a value within a legal context, so that 'expert' encompasses an interface between scientific activity and the public. This interface is characterised as having actors moving through the different layers, for example, experts versus non-experts, scientific research versus public debates. Although an expert was traditionally defined within an individual or group of individuals, Cambrosio et al (1992) argue that 'expert knowledge' is the property of a network and that individuals with tacit and formal knowledge must become part of a network to function as part of a body of expertise.

Eyal (2013) took up this argument by analysing how different forms of expertise have developed through the use of "networks which bring together objects, actors, techniques, devices and institutional and spatial arrangements" (Eyal, 2013: 873). She used this analysis to explain the history of professional approaches to autism during the twentieth century. This has changed from professionals assuming that their knowledge, skills and expertise have to inform how to 'treat' autism to a greater acknowledgement of the knowledge, skills and expertise that people with autism and their families have, which is key to developing policies and services that meet the needs of this community (Eyal, 2013; Silberman, 2016). Eyal shows that this process of what can be described as co-production or co-creation leads to a strengthening of the professionals' expertise even if the expert's autonomy may appear diminished.

Although the term expert has already been defined above as 'to try' and 'to do', Collins (2014) provides an analysis that can help to inform the future relationship between democratic professionals and public service users which recognises that service users have greater access to much information and certain types of knowledge. Collins distinguishes between two types of 'ubiquitous expertise' – ubiquitous tacit knowledge and specialist tacit knowledge – the former covering knowledge acquired by growing up in a society and through reading and other media, which he calls 'beer mat knowledge'. This is popular understanding and primary source knowledge, which does not necessarily require contact with experts. In contrast, specialist tacit knowledge is often learnt through work or apprenticeship/ study and is of two types: I: acquired by participating in an expert community but without contributing to the creation of new expert knowledge; 2: contributory expertise which involves the creation of new knowledge and expertise. This detailed definition of expertise acknowledges a wider range of expertise than the usual limited meaning of the concept, some of it is accumulated by growing up in a society, but Collins recognises that expertise has to be created and built up.

Seeing different forms of expertise as points on a continuum of expertise can help the democratic professional to understand how expertise is constructed and the role of networks in the creation of expertise. It can inform the decision about who should be in a network and how to widen networks, thus creating a more sensitive and nuanced type of expertise. The processes that result in expertise being created have to be better understood and a greater openness to a much wider group of stakeholders who contribute to the formation of expertise, rather than just assuming that only experts are involved. Identifying how knowledge is created to answer specific problems also raises the need to address why certain problems are addressed and others ignored.

Another reason for the current distrust of experts can be understood as having been informed by the way in which science and public policy interact. There is a growing research literature which explores critically the relationships between citizens and scientific experts in the formulation, design and implementation of public policies. Writing in 2005, Sheila Jasanoff pointed out:

> At stake, therefore, is a deeper right to define how, when, by whom, and to what extent science will be integrated into the solution of public problems, and who, indeed, will frame those problems in the first place. (Jasanoff, 2005: 210)

This is clearly a political process. The use of social networks which create knowledge and expertise must be understood in relation to the mechanisms which draw different individuals and groups into the network. The example of how the UK National Institute for Clinical and Public Health Excellence (NICE) develops guidelines on the use of drugs and other treatments with the involvement of lay people shows some of the problems in developing a democratic process. In 2014, the National Institute for Clinical and Public Health Excellence published 'Developing NICE guidelines: the manual', which set out the processes and procedures used to development NICE guidelines. Stakeholders, defined as "organisations with an interest in a particular guideline topic.... may represent people whose practice or care is directly affected by the guideline" (NICE, 2014: 24), play an essential role in this process. They are encouraged to become involved in all stages of the process, which may be commenting on drafts, providing evidence and supporting the implementation of the guidelines.

Although this process has become more inclusive since NICE was founded in 1999 with a very wide range of stakeholders now involved in developing a set of guidelines, these are mostly national organisations that represent but do not directly involve patients, families or carers. They complement national organisations that represent health and social care practitioners, public sector providers and commissioners of services, voluntary and other providers of services, companies manufacturing drugs, medical devices, research organisations and government and statutory agencies. There are different levels of resources available to many of these stakeholders, with patient organisations probably having much less access to the information required to operate effectively within this process.

Beebeejaun et al (2015) provide a critique of current research governance which presents communities as 'vulnerable subjects'. They show that using the concept of 'public value' would be a more constructive way of viewing research which would move away from the aim of minimising harm to communities. Instead it would engage communities in ways that allow them to work with researchers to "generate knowledge and informed action" (Kesby, 2007; 2013). Public value has emerged as a way of rebuilding the legitimacy of public institutions (Goss, 2001). The challenging of conventional forms of research governance can also be placed in the context of questioning how knowledge is constructed by institutions (Freire, 1970).

The concept of co-production of knowledge has evolved from a wider dissatisfaction with forms of participation to recognition that knowledge should be constructed so that one form of knowledge is not favoured over another one. This approach encourages a more reflexive form of research where academic researchers can work with members of communities to create knowledge and research together instead of communities being informants to research. This is not an easy process to construct and needs new ways of thinking together. Pohl et al (2010) suggest the creation of a 'boundary space' which brings the different worlds of academic research and communities together, which they described as separate "thought collectives". It should not be a question of enabling community members to understand academic research but be about creating a "dialogue on equal terms between thought collectives" (Pohl et al, 2010: 271). This approach can also contribute to a changing role for universities in the creation of public value and their relationship with local communities (Burawoy, 2005; Streek, 2016).

An example of how the combined energy of grassroots health activists, civil society organizations and academic institutions from around the world, particularly from low- and middle-income countries are playing an important role in new systems of global health governance can be seen in the case of the People's Health Movement (PHM), set up in 2000 at the first People's Health Assembly in Bangladesh. The People's Health Movement (PHM) is strongly critical of public–private partnerships and the involvement of charitable foundations, for example, the Bill and Melinda Gates Foundation, in global health, but PHM is also a loose network of individuals and advocacy groups which operate within policy networks, publishing research and being part of peer-reviewed publishing as well as mobilising networks of grassroots activists. De Leeuw et al (2013) argue that changes in global health governance are a reflection of the engagement of diverse multi-level stakeholders attempting to address the determinants of health (de Leeuw et al, 2013: 104).

Technology, expertise and public services

Susskind and Susskind (2015) argue that new technologies are already transforming the work of professionals so that their traditional professional role as gatekeepers to privileged knowledge is no longer needed. The access that many public service users have to the Internet and a vast amount of information provides many more people with information about their conditions, health and lives. This access to large amounts of information makes the challenge to professional judgements more intense.

This could be described as part of a more democratic process, but evidence of recent uses of personal digital data in election campaigns have shown that the Internet does not operate as part of a politically neutral or democratic process. The global technology companies that provide access to the Internet have strong agendas that do not support collective forms of citizen action and freedom but are promoting and supporting a strongly individualistic world, where each individual will be expected to have responsibility for their own well-being and survival (Morozov, 2015). The rejection of the views of professionals and experts which is coupled with an increased access to information through the Internet and social media needs to be seen in relation to the position of global companies that provide access to this information. However, it requires action by democratic professionals and broader-based campaigns to create a public digital space that is democratic. Making the battle for democratic control of the Internet part of democratic professionalism strengthens the argument that democratic digital rights must be recognised as part of the wider structures of society, including public services.

There is an important gender dimension in relation to digital technology. Women are a minority in the workforce of IT and global technology companies, and there is evidence to show that many of the behavioural models which inform digital technology are based on predominantly male behaviours. There is an urgent need for women to have a stronger influence over the development and application of digital technologies. If democratic professionals, many of whom will be women, start to engage in the processes of shaping the application of digital technologies to meet the goals of public services, this will help to provide a stronger recognition of the needs of women. It is another example of how an awareness of plurality must inform the application of digital technologies to public services.

The search to democratise the development and production of new technologies has similar motivations to the recent calls for a global governance to control technological decisions (Jasanoff, 2005, 2016). It is this complex, and in many ways still undefined area, that democratic professionals will have to negotiate when looking at diverse forms of knowledge and skills and rethinking their own roles. They should also try to help citizens and users negotiate and counter the focus on individualism thus promoting a more public, collective view of technology in society. Jasanoff (2016) discusses the nature of knowledge and expertise and the inequalities of access to technological knowledge. She sees it as both an unresolved ethical issue and a political barrier to a "just governance of technological innovation" (Jasanoff, 2016: 256). The underlying theme of her book *The Ethics of Invention* was how to address inequalities between individuals and companies which develop new technological products and the increasingly large populations who are likely to be affected by technological change. A new form of global governance is needed, but this will depend on acknowledging that:

> Institutional deficiencies, unequal resources and complacent storytelling hamper profound reflections on intersection and mutual influence of technology and human values. (Jasanoff, 2016: 265)

An example of how citizens and democratic professionals have come together to examine new technologies can be seen in the creation of the Network for the Social Evaluation of Technologies in Latin America (*Red Tecla*), which was formed in 2006 to look at the impact of new technologies on society. Members recognised that the social, economic and environmental impact of new technologies took place long after these products entered the market. There is rarely any evaluation or regulation of new technologies and they are often promoted as technical solutions to wider environmental or climate change crises.

Red Tecla argues that public evaluation of technologies has a long history in international governance, for example, Agenda 21, Chapter 34 (1992), establishes a "rational transfer" of technology and foresees forms of evaluation. *Red Tecla* aims to:

- reflect on the science and technology and the context within which it is developed in order to understand the goals and logic of these new technologies and to stimulate debate beyond scientific fields in order to integrate diverse systems of knowledge;
- map technological criticisms by drawing on the extensive criticisms and evaluations done by organisations and movements;
- review the technological 'horizon' to be able to anticipate the significance of new technologies and their social, economic and environmental impacts; and
- establish a dialogue with policy makers bringing *Red Tecla* findings to the public arena (*Red Tecla*, 2018). It recognises that democratic assessment of technologies must operate at local, national and international levels and has to bring together different types of expertise in a way that respects and values each type.

This has wider implications for how citizens and professionals can interact democratically and how technology can be used to address societal problems rather than contribute to company profits. Cooley (1987) in '*Architect or Bee? The human/technology relationship*' wrote presciently about how the relationship between people, workers and technology needed to change so that it became more centred on the needs of society or 'human-centred technology (Cooley, 1987).

Designing public services with democratically created expertise

As part of the process of developing a more open approach to knowledge and skills, democratic professionals have started to work with services users and other stakeholders in ways that acknowledge that expertise has to be shared and valued. User movements, for example, people living with physical and mental disabilities, have argued consistently over the last four decades that the knowledge and experience of service users has to be valued. But this must be more than just a question of democratic professionals listening to different 'voices'.

Understanding the role that different types of knowledge and skills and the subsequent creation of diverse types of expertise play in the delivery of public services will help to show how to share and draw from diverse forms of expertise. Analysing current examples of how democratic professionals are starting to deal with knowledge and skills in ways which acknowledge and respect service users and disadvantaged communities will show some of the approaches that can be used.

These issues are not new and public professionals have been trying to answer them for many years. In Germany, after 1968, there was a questioning of the then Fordist approach to welfare, which was characterised as being functional, paternalist and rational. New social and political movements demanded increased citizen participation in social transformation processes (Lorenz, 2008). Within universities, the concept of social pedagogy, already well established in Germany, developed as a result of critical discussions about the relationship of the individual and society, led by Klaus Mollenhauer, who wanted to de-institutionalise pedagogic thinking and keep it focused on practical tasks which were the result of people trying to address "difficult life situations" (Lorenz, 2008: 639). He used the concept of the "lifeworld" to describe the coping abilities that clients had available, but which were "different from the world professionals occupy and whose values they often seek to impose" (Lorenz, 2008: 639).

Although the German system of social welfare has been subject to public sector reforms, which have made the social services professionals subject to restructuring, targets and a managerial agenda, Lorenz argued that social work and social pedagogy can contribute to a new form of social solidarity which will depend on professionals having an understanding of these 'life worlds' (Lorenz, 2008: 640-641). Mollenhauer and Lorenz argued that social professionals needed to understand the lifeworld of their clients and this approach can be linked to the development of democratic professionals in relation to the acquisition and use of knowledge and skills.

Pamela Fisher (2016) at a meeting of the 'Democratic Professionalism in Mental Health Services' research project argued for a 'decolonisation' of knowledge, informed by making a connection between post-colonial theory and co-production. She felt that service user perspectives are often not taken seriously as legitimate forms of knowledge. Fisher and Lees (2015) argued that "not only that service users should be heard, but also that their voices should carry the power to effect real changes" (Fisher and Lees, 2015: 10). The concept of the de-colonisation of knowledge has been widely used in relation to the oppression and suppression of history and knowledge of peoples who were colonised. There are parallels in the way in which the knowledge and expertise of public service users is often ignored and not valued in public service delivery, and this can be seen as a form of colonisation. If knowledge and skills are to be reviewed and reconsidered, thinking of the processes as being similar to the rethinking that has taken place in history, geography and literature may provide some guidance for democratic professionals.

New arrangements for creating and sharing knowledge in a more democratic way are needed and public sector professionals will have to use a wider range of techniques to support clients in interpreting and applying knowledge. An example of how mental health professionals are addressing some of these issues within a framework of democratic professionalism can be seen in a recent series of seminars organised as part of the 'Democratic Professionalism in Mental Health Services Research Project' part of an ESRC seminar series 'Re-imagining Professionalism in Mental Health: towards co-production' held at the University of Leeds on the 5 January 2016. The seminar was informed by the view that "Our starting point is that professionalism should be informed by the principle of authentic power-sharing between service users, carers and professionals" (Democratic Professionalism and Mental Health Workshop, 2016).

The discussions that resulted from a desire to work in a more democratic way indicate some of the types of debate that must take place when professionals start to question how their practice can be more democratic. One issue of pursuing a more democratic professionalism is how to 'embed' it into organisational cultures. A discussion about what professionalism should encompass led to questions about "what should constitute professionalism and whether the definition should be expanded to include services users, informal carers and peer support workers". One participant (Scott Bell) pointed out that co-productive relationships should involve mutuality and reciprocity but the term 'user-led' tended to place more responsibility for recovery on the service user. Other participants argued that 'user-led' still maintains an oppressive relationship between service users and service providers. A more appropriate term within democratic professionalism might be a model of "recovery together". This is a therapeutic approach which:

> imagines recovery as a process of growth and development, enabling recovery to be found in ways that could not be anticipated at the outset. Crucially, it involves a democratic relationship between service users and practitioners. (Fisher and Lees, 2015: 10)

However, the term 'recovery together' has been criticised as placing most of the responsibility for getting better onto the service user and excuses or hides the limited treatments available to service users because of lack of funding of mental health services. It shows the difficulties in developing more democratic ways of working between service users and public professionals in times of austerity.

Although citizens often have extensive knowledge that is rarely drawn on in the delivery of public services, there are also sources of specialist tacit knowledge which professionals will continue to have a role in interpreting for services users. The way in which this specialist tacit knowledge is made accessible to patients, clients and service users is important, so that the sharing of this expertise is done in a way which empowers clients to ask questions and make their own judgements. One of the challenges facing democratic professionals is how to balance their search for diverse sources of expertise with a continued questioning and valuing of their own expertise. Digitalisation is beginning to change some aspects of this relationship. X-rays can be digitally interpreted, although the results will still have to be given to the patient by a healthcare professional.

This approach can be applied to nursing and shows the type of changes which need to take place for public professionals to start to operate in a democratic way. A nurse trade unionist recognised that there are new forms of professionalism evolving, particularly influenced by new systems of professional education and training (Lethbridge, 2015). He was particularly interested in the concept of democratic professionalism, and proceeded to make links to recent trade union work. His union was taking a lead in public and patient participation issues, which address ways in which patients and citizens can participate in health services.

> How to empower the union to contribute to this and combined with student issues over the next 10 years will be critical... these are huge issues still to plan for and are about relationships between professionals and society. Democratic professionalism will only happen if these processes start up. There is a more active participation and confidence of nurses in training at individual level and at group level. A more comprehensive view of democracy and democratic professionals and criticisms that professionals get – so must admit where it has gone wrong and how to engage in the future. (Lethbridge, 2015, 230)

This is important if professional protectionism and self-interest are to be challenged. Professionals need to admit where they went wrong but require confidence in order to be able to do this. Nurse education now teaches ethics and the personalisation of care and the exploration of these topics in training help to make nurses less apprehensive about being challenged. Patients have access to more information from the Internet but there is still a way to go before relationships between nurse and patient become more complementary. Education has to play a role in this change.

Returning to Arendt's *vita activa*, action in this context means taking a much more proactive approach to understanding other forms of knowledge and accepting their validity. Starting from the point of view of 'action' can help to examine how knowledge and skills are approached in the processes of labour and work. Taking the example of the 'labour' dimension of public services, which are the routine and often less valued part of public services, how are knowledge, skills and expertise built up? Is the contribution of service users, families and local communities to this knowledge acknowledged? If a more diverse approach to the knowledge, skills and expertise of other stakeholders was taken, how would the delivery of the services change and how would the role of the public professionals change? The example of a Leeds Social Services initiative which aims to value the knowledge and expertise of the families of children who are either in the 'care' of the local authority or at risk of being taken into 'care' shows how a different approach results in different types of decisions about children.

Recognising family expertise

There is a long tradition of radical social work but the introduction of public management reforms has forced social workers to think in new and more creative ways about how to work with their clients in different and more democratic ways. Ferguson (2009) argued that user movements, for example, the disability movement, have influenced many progressive service developments.

An example of how the use of caring expertise can be made more democratic is seen in the way in which Leeds Social Services are trying to value the knowledge and skills of families in relation to care of a child, described as their 'Family Valued' programme. As with mental health services, even after fifty years of campaigning by family rights groups, the power of public professionals to take away a child from her/his parents continues to be deeply contested, although the rights of parents are now more widely recognised in this process, which allows them to challenge decisions. Based on a belief that the decisions within the care system are not always informed by a family approach, the 'Family Valued' programme aims to value the knowledge, skills and experience of caring within the wider family in making a decision, using a restorative approach. Leeds Social Services defines restorative practice as:

> A term used to describe a way of behaving which helps to build and maintain healthy relationships, resolve difficulties and repair harm where there has been conflict... describes a 'way of being' when communicating and resolving difficulties. Restorative practices enable those who work with children and families to focus upon building relationships that create change. Creating change sometimes requires challenge as well as support. (Leeds City Council, 2018)

The recognition that family care is significant starts to value expertise which is often seen as predominantly women's expertise. The significance of this cannot be underestimated. This is one way of interpreting plurality, which should inform all public services.

This new way of working requires public professionals to be trained so that they can operate in a different way, but this should be seen in the context of the valuing of women's expertise in a profession which is predominantly female. Professionals and practitioners are being trained to use restorative techniques to work with children, young people and families to help them find their own solutions safely and appropriately to problems in order to avoid a social work intervention. They provide "staff with a range of language, behaviours and tools that strengthen their relationships with children, young people and families, empowering them to share responsibility and support positive change." Families are supported to make an alternative plan before a child is taken into the care of the local authority. Multi-agency practitioners are being trained in restorative techniques to work with families.

The success of this approach depends not just on skills training for public professionals but in incorporating democratic elements into the organisation of space. The decisions about how space is organised, where people sit and how meetings are run are all democratic decisions. For example, meetings:

Are held in circles, rather than around tables, to remove physical and psychological barriers between people. Meetings may be facilitated by skilled staff to create an environment where those attending can share their thoughts and feelings in a way which is constructive. The focus of these meetings may be to build relationships, solve specific problems or repair harm where there has been conflict. (Leeds City Council, 2018)

Leeds Social Services is also using Family Group Conferencing as a way of working with families and sometimes as an alternative to an initial child protection conference. This approach draws extended families and staff together, "in a decision-making circle to consider risks and concerns about their children. The family have private family time to create a plan that fits in with their individual dynamics, and enables family leadership in what would otherwise be a professionalised planning process" (Leeds City Council, 2018).

The family group conference, originally developed in New Zealand, was introduced into England and Wales by the Family Rights Group (FRG), a not-for-profit organisation set up in 1974 to support the rights of parents to question the power of social workers to take children into the 'care' of the local authority. FRG campaigns for the rights of parents to be recognised in decisions about whether a child should be taken into the 'looked after care' of the local authority. It also runs the National Family Group Conference Network as part of its role in introducing new democratic practices to departments of social services. Family group conferences are not just another technique for public professionals to use when working with families (FGC). The family has to make a decision about having an FGC and the terms in which an FGC takes place are subject to agreement with the family.

Whether or not a family group conference takes place is a decision made by the family. Under no circumstances can a family be made or forced to have a family group conference. (Family Rights Group, 2018)

Family Group Conferences are an example of a tool that has been developed so that families can work with social workers in a more democratic way.

Catherine Hasted (2012), the chief operating officer at Daybreak, a voluntary organisation focusing on the delivery of family group conferences, recounts her experience of a family group conference.

> Sitting in the middle of a family group conference, for the first time, felt like gate crashing a family party. It was noisy, children were chatting and playing and there was a constant flow of tea and coffee. As chaotic as it sounds, there was magic at work. The family reconnected, ready to come together to tackle the serious concerns expressed by baby Jake's social worker.
>
> The bottom line was clear, Jake's older sibling had been taken into care from birth, if a safe plan could not be found for Jake then history would repeat itself. But the referring social worker could see that mum was back on track, she loved her child, had the support of her family and wanted to make it work.
>
> Both sides of the family came together, many of them had never even met each other before but they shared a joint purpose and a feeling of responsibility towards this little boy. Gradually I saw a change in body language; the family were animated and engaged. Jake took centre stage; you could feel his mum bursting with pride at the fuss being made of her son.
>
> Then we were asked to leave the room and leave the family to it. What went on during those two hours will only ever be known by the family, they shared private information, deep family history and were more open and honest than they could ever hope to be in front of professionals.
>
> When the family presented the plan to Jake's social worker, it was mum who stood at the front with a flip chart, standing her ground to answer questions and

defend the plan. What a change from the hunched teenager, hiding behind her mobile phone at the beginning of the day. Two hours later Jake left the room with his mum, her family and a safe plan of action agreed there and then by the social worker. I left that first meeting with admiration for the family and the professionals. (Hasted, 2012)

This account of a family group conference highlights the empowering effect that it had on the whole family, bringing it together for the first time. It also had a transforming effect on the young mother. She was able to argue and defend the plan drawn up by the family, which contributed to her own empowerment.

Everyone involved in an FRC has to have some training and support. The use of the technique is facilitated by the Family Group Conference Service and over 70% of local authorities now have a Family Group Conference Service which will arrange and facilitate family group conferences.

To use a family group conference effectively involves democratic professionals working in different ways and questioning their own assumptions. It is not just about knowledge and expertise though, the way in which space is used and the openness around it makes a difference to the power of families and children to shape decisions. Putting plurality into action has to operate at different levels of social exchanges, which include physical and emotional spaces.

Risk assessment

Assessment of risk is one of the so-called professional 'skills' that public professionals have to use in relation to clients and service users. One of the critical views of risk assessment in public services is the extent to which the knowledge, skills and expertise of service users and clients are taken into consideration when making a judgement which will affect an individual or family.

One of the professional issues that underpin many public services involves the assessment by professionals of behaviours, which are considered to be a risk to the individual, family or wider community. Risk assessment is often at the heart of how a public professional makes a decision. Often subject to management targets, goals and the threat of the loss of a professional licence, public professionals are not independent providers in this complex process of how the state delivers public services for the benefit of citizens as well as providing public protection.

A project which has been developed as a result of discussions about democratic professionalism within mental health services shows how the professional skill of risk assessment can be subjected to a democratic lens.

Leanne Winfield, a service user, provided an account of the 'The Multi-Agency Clinical Risk Training Project', set up in 2016 by the Leeds and York Partnership NHS Foundation Trust to make training in clinical risk more relevant and consistent between sectors. It was open to staff from voluntary and statutory organisations, carers and service users. She explained that the project started with a series of workshops, which were "open to a wide range of staff from various statutory and voluntary organisations, carers, and service users, to look at the issue of clinical risk training" (Winfield, 2016). The workshops started by looking at existing training in clinical risk which was provided by different agencies and organisations. They were looking for more relevance and consistency between NHS, adult social care and voluntary sectors. These workshops generated many ideas. A project steering group was set up which "co-produced a training package, drawing on our own personal experiences and the themes that resulted from the workshops" and worked as an equal partner in planning and delivering the workshops. A series of workshops informed by this training package and made by participants who were service users, carers and service providers:

> prompted the attendees to take a broader look at the concept of 'risk', and their own experiences – both within and outside their professional roles. (Winfield, 2016)

The basis of the training was to look at two real-life case studies, which detailed the experiences of Leanne Winfield and a second service user. The workshop participants were asked to imagine "What would you do?" After they outlined what they would do, the two service users gave an account of what actually happened. Leanne Winfield commented that:

> It was great to be recognised as equals regardless of either being Experts by Learning or Experts by Experience. Hopefully our success can inspire future projects, and make a strong case for what can be achieved with co-production. (Winfield, 2016)

This project involved the use of public pedagogy, where teaching and learning by democratic professionals, citizens and services users took place together with sharing of the knowledge and expertise that was created. This again shows how plurality can be put into practice. It draws on different types of expertise, many of them held by women and undervalued by society.

Design for carbon reduction

Another example of how democratic professionals worked with local community groups shows that different approaches to public pedagogy are needed in different settings. Working democratically also requires participants in the process to receive some training. The theme of 'public and collaborative' was proposed by Ezio Mantini and colleagues at Parsons, the New School for Design, based in New York, in September 2011 to try and answer the design questions:

> How are emerging social networks meeting public services and innovation policies? And vice versa, how can public services and innovation policies trigger, empower and direct the emerging social networks? (Thorpe and Gamman, 2013: 52)

A partnership between the University of the Arts London, which included BA Product Design students and MA Applied Imagination students, Camden Council and local community groups was one of the initiatives inspired by these questions. The concept of 'socially responsive design' is defined as:

> a diverse set of design activities which, as design researchers, we engage in with diverse actors that prioritize social goals and needs over those of the market. (Thorpe and Gamman, 2013: 53)

Camden Council approached the University of the Arts, London (UAL) in 2013 to create a practice-based research project to help change the behaviour of people to reduce carbon emissions by exploring new ways of living and working in Camden. Although three stakeholder groups had been identified, UAL felt that the council residents were the best way of meeting the 'Public and Collaborative' brief. Camden Council also has a 'green zone' initiative targeting 30 neighbourhoods to increase take-up of 75 different actions related to reducing carbon emissions. UAL suggested that these two initiatives should be addressed together. Within UAL, the Product Design course wanted to find a 'social innovation-themed client project' for their graduating students.

UAL worked with Camden Council and created a strategy to identify and communicate with community groups "in ways which would be accessible to them" by using a weblog, and asked the council to contact their Green Zones representatives to inform them of the weblog. This was a slow process. Preparing the students for this project required some reorientation, because the students had studied product design but did not necessarily have experience of working with local communities. Many students were unsure of how to work collaboratively with local people to identify the product design opportunities. They had little experience of designing a service as opposed to designing a product. UAL had to teach the students these skills by getting them to identify existing projects and map them as product service systems. Students developed a series of product proposals which addressed ways of changing behaviours and used them to start talking to community groups about the project brief.

The process of trying to prepare students for a fundamentally different way of approaching a design brief was slow and not always successful. However, the involvement of students from an MA Applied Imagination course drew in some relevant skills and experiences and provided peer support for the BA students. Community engagement after students had managed to refine their ideas, thoughts and proposals was rich, although did not always take the form of a co-design workshop as had been planned. Many of the projects used a user-centred design methodology rather than a co-design approach. Matching community expectations within the limitations of student deadlines was difficult.

One of the main conclusions drawn was the importance of clarifying "what necessary community 'expertise' means" in the context of a design project and to what extent it is found within the communities involved in the project.

> Whilst community members are often 'experts' of their own experience and this experience is essential to appropriate collaborative design outcomes, our experience is that specialist expertise and research is often needed to progress projects at this scoping stage and this is not always located in community groups. (Thorpe and Gamman, 2013: 60)

Other learning recognised that the set-up phase with the community was central to the success of the project and the development of dialogue in early phases made subsequent processes of co-design easier. As a result of the project more community conversations started which would not have occurred without the project. Perhaps the most important learning for Camden Council was that design is not something that happens at the end of a process but is:

> An approach that can be utilized to identify what policy are necessary to enable and facilitate desirable change within communities… design can fulfill a role in helping communities better articulate and engage with definition of policy agendas as well as development and delivery of policy recommendations. (Thorpe and Gamman, 2013: 64)

This example focused on the design and creation of services for saving water, compost delivery and electric car management as well as services to support food growing and gaining access to local and seasonal food, which will address public policy issues. There was extensive learning from everyone involved. This has contributed to a much longer learning process, but emphasises the importance of placing design within a democratic context.

The process of learning which took place between all groups was often slow and difficult. It provides another view of how plurality can be implemented, but it shows that the skills of working collaboratively cannot be assumed to exist. Although the experience of the project will have given students increased confidence in working with diverse groups, their lack of confidence at the beginning of the project shows that higher education should incorporate training to work with diverse groups into courses. This should be underpinned by the supporting students to use plurality as one of a set of principles to inform their work.

New universities

Many of these examples of how democratic professionalism has been put into practice show that different forms of public pedagogy have to inform the support and training needed. This not only has implications for specific public services but should impact on the work of higher education institutions which contribute to the training of democratic professionals. This section looks at two examples of new 'universities' which incorporate democratic principles in the way in which they are run.

One example of how higher education can start to think and to act critically is the creation of a cooperative university at the University of Lincoln. The content of discussions that led to a planned cooperative university illustrates some of the issues that have emerged as part of this process. In higher education, the challenge of how to share knowledge democratically within an increasingly marketised system is a major problem for democratic professionals working within universities. Universities now have to deal with the consequences of making students into consumers, which affects relationships within institutions, but also makes the implementation of a pluralist approach more difficult. A response to this problem was created by Neary and Winn (2009) who developed the concept of the 'Student as Producer' as a central strategy in future higher education, which recognises that both students and academics are involved as academic workers in the production of critical-practical knowledge. This interpretation of plurality draws together groups within the university as well as potentially involving other interest groups outside it.

The Social Science Centre (SSC) in Lincoln was created with the 'Student as Producer' informing the pedagogy and is technically a separate organisation from the University of Lincoln although there are close links. Students work with academics on research projects and create space which supports a democratic relationship between academics and students. They work together on co-designing curricula, developing research projects and a recognition that academics and students have much to learn from each other. The experience of the SSC had found that the relationships between students, academics, administrators and support workers were central and had to be:

> grounded in a constitutional framework that confronts issues of power, difference and desire, as well as (in) equalities, while at the same time recognising the importance of deliberative leadership. (Neary and Winn, 2017: 91)

The curriculum has to be open and enquiring with no learning outcomes defined at the beginning of the process, in contrast to mainstream university courses, although some sense of progress and structure was required. The content of the curriculum had to be grounded in the lives of members and the communities, where the cooperative is located. Topics cover housing, health, employment and other issues and the curriculum reflected cooperative society – critical political economy, history of the workers movement, working class intellectuality and philosophy, gender studies, linking national and social sciences as different forms of knowledge. This has successful implemented a strategy of plurality into a new form of university. A participatory action project was created to develop a framework for higher education based on a model of the cooperative. The research group included members of the Social Science Centre, researchers of cooperative enterprise, historians, legal specialists, online educators, working members of cooperatives and academics and students involved in the free university movement and supportive organisations and the Cooperative College. Five workshops (48 participants) and five on-line focus groups gathered ideas and views on what a cooperative university should encompass. Its subsequent plans for setting up a cooperative university shows how re-thinking of higher education can begin. Exploring new ways of teaching and learning and developing systems of governance that are inclusive provided a foundation for the plans for a cooperative university.

Interviewees for the participatory action project saw pedagogy as a 'social-human relationship' and so it should be seen as an organisational pillar. They felt that "care for others can itself be pedagogic" and that pedagogy has to be focused on the relationship between teacher and student rather than being student-centred or knowledge-centred. A teacher was described as "researchers with time for others, inspiring students to undertake their own research" (Neary and Winn, 2017: 99). Although the traditions of 'popular' and 'critical' pedagogies were acknowledged as having informed the SSC, interviewees felt it important to go beyond these and revise these progressive forms of teaching and learning. They wanted to develop a pedagogy which was a process of consensus decision-making among members.

> The responsibility of active membership and participation is itself a form of pedagogy and 'people have to enter the process with a willingness to be transformed and to change their attitudes and behaviour'. (Neary and Winn, 2017: 99)

The Cooperative University has only recently been set up but the process of setting it up, building on the work of the

Social Science Centre has shown some of the learning that needs to take place when setting up a more democratic educational structure.

A second example of another type of university also challenges the conventional student-lecturer relationship. The Silent University is another way of exploring knowledge and skills development through the creation of a "solidarity based knowledge exchange platform by refugees, asylum seekers and migrants" (Silent University, 2012a). It was set up by Ahmet Öğüt, an artist, working on a year-long residency at the Tate Gallery in partnership with the Delfina Foundation. He worked with a group of lecturers, consultants and research fellows who had all experienced the process of seeking asylum and migration, which had resulted in them being unable to use their skills and knowledge because their qualifications are not recognised in their new country of residence. Each group works on course development related to their qualifications, specific research on themes related to asylum, refugees and migrants as well as reflecting on what it means to be an asylum seeker, refugee and migrant.

The Silent University aims to reactivate the knowledge of these groups who are unable to use their skills or professional training in the UK because of the extent of their professional work is determined by their legal status. Even more unusually, the Silent University aims to:

> challenge the idea of silence as a passive state, and explore its powerful potential through performance, writing and group reflection... to make apparent the systemic failure and loss of skills and knowledge experienced through the silencing process of people seeking asylum. (Silent University, 2012a)

Described as 'Towards a Transversal Pedagogy', the Silent University has drawn up 14 principles and demands. As well as demanding the right to educate and the immediate recognition of the academic backgrounds of asylum seekers and refugees, it also questions the nature of contemporary education and states:

>Artistic pedagogical practices need to be emancipated from commonly used terminologies such as 'projects' and 'workshops'... Pedagogic practices must be based on long-term engagement, commitment and determination... Revolution of decolonising pedagogies. (Silent University, 2012a)

The concept of silence is central to the work and is described by its founder, Ahmet Ögüt, as:

>It is a poetic protest. It is a functional tool. It is about exchanging positions through empathy. It is a consciously delayed exchange. It is a currency. (Silent University, 2012b: 7)

The University aims to address and reactivate the knowledge of the participants and make the exchange process mutually beneficial by inventing alternative currencies, in place of money or free voluntary service. The Silent University was set up in London in 2012 in collaboration with Delfina Foundation and Tate and later hosted by The Showroom. It has expanded to several countries since then, including Germany, Sweden, Jordan and Greece. This is an important example in that it drew people who were unable to use their own expertise and created a way of expressing it in a supportive environment. This is another example of how an awareness of plurality can be put into practice.

Conclusion

One of the recurring themes in these examples and case studies is the use of language and how it needs to change to reflect changes in the balance of power between service users and public professionals. This means moving away from the language of consumerism and new public management and rethinking language for more democratic public services. Professionals in social work and mental health services are exploring ways of working a ways that are more democratic and equal with families and service users. They show that to adopt a more democratic approach, requires looking at the types of language used, facilitating communication, information-sharing and decision-making and making changes to professional practices. The term 'co-production' is not necessarily an empowering way of redefining relationships. If there is a greater understanding and valuing of different types of experience it may result in the rejection of the term professional.

The use of a pluralist perspective has been able to value many areas of women's caring expertise in the household which either remain hidden or unacknowledged. There are connections which need to be made between the process of valuing women's expertise and the recognition that many public professionals are women. What are the dynamics which accompany these transformative processes?

The creation of the Silent University by refugees and migrants in order to use their professional expertise is just one example of how the creation of a plurality within learning environments can start to address ways of making diverse histories and perspectives more widely recognised. Silence is used in a positive way to show the potential of silenced voices.

Building on a more inclusive understanding of knowledge, skills and expertise, the next chapter will look at the contribution that democratic professionals can make to widen the public sphere. This will explore how democratic professionals can, not just identify a wider range of publics, but find ways of facilitating their inclusion into public services.

4

Developing an inclusive public sphere

The last chapter (Identifying diverse sources of expertise) discussed how a democratic professional can acknowledge and understand different sources of knowledge, skills and expertise. This may result in the identification of many different publics, which public services have to serve. Valuing diverse forms of expertise has to be informed by a sense of respect which will inform any action taken. Respecting services users by listening, supporting, empowering and ultimately working towards greater equality and mutual understanding has to be a central function of democratic professionals, but this will depend on developing different ways of working with service users.

Respecting services users is closely related to acting with integrity. Mayer (1995) identified integrity as a component of trust. Democratic professionals will have to have a self-awareness of their own values, prejudices, beliefs, limitations and fallibility (Taubman, 2013), which involves extensive reflection on professional practice and honesty about professional limitations. It highlights some of the tensions that public professionals operating within public sector reforms will experience when their professional judgement is challenged by a management agenda.

Even before the introduction of management driven systems, public professionals had been questioning their own judgements in relation to the needs of their clients and patients, for example, nurses questioning the power relationships between doctors, nurses and patients. Matthew Pianalto (2012) in 'Integrity and Struggle' in the journal *Philosophia* developed the concept of practical integrity, which he defined as for those who "must confront, manage and control factors that give rise to various kinds of inner conflict" (Pianalto, 2012: 335). This sums up some of the conflicts that democratic professionals may experience, which emerge when trying to operate with integrity. These are not easy processes to deal with at any time but during a period when budgets for public services are being reduced and cost-reduction drives new approaches, they provide profound professional challenges.

The terms respect, integrity and trust feature strongly in attempts to improve governance in public services, for example, the Code of Practice for the General Social Care Council (2010) which includes "respect the rights of services users whilst seeking to ensure that their behaviour does not harm themselves or other people". There is much more widespread questioning of the integrity of public professionals as a result of public sector reforms. Both respect and integrity are part of the process of questioning how public professionals work with services users. There is an underlying management assumption that public professionals do not always respect service users, and so their professional integrity is questioned. Yet, some of the results of public sector reforms result in public professionals being unable to operate with professional integrity because of the conflicts between professional and management judgements.

This chapter will explore how democratic professionals can both respect service users and act with professional and personal integrity. Arendt emphasized the importance of creating a public realm or sphere which has a long-term perspective, a sense of permanence and the capacity to gather people together (Arendt, 1958: 55). This book argues that public services are delivered in such a public sphere and that a critical appreciation of how this public sphere is created and maintained must be at the heart of public service delivery. This requires greater respect and integrity. Before the democratic professional can start to take action to strengthen the public sphere, they will have to revisit the concept of the public interest. An inclusive understanding of the public interest underpins any form of respect shown to service users and will inform democratic professionals how to maintain their own integrity.

Public interest

The concept of the public interest is a central issue in political philosophy. The transformation of the interests of many people into a common good has been seen as a central part of the political process. Thomas Aquinas defined the "common good" as the purpose of government and law. Aristotle identified the difference between the right constitution 'in the common interest' and the wrong constitution in the 'interests of rulers'. Jean-Jacques Rousseau defined the "common good" as the general will and purpose of government.

In a more tangible form, public interest can be seen as the shared interests of different levels of government. It may mean shared values or a balance of interests. Sometimes it is used as a moral standard for public action or in the 'best' interests of society. All attempts to define the public interest have to bring together individual interests in society into a common, public and general good, which encapsulates and transcends each individual interest. It can also be about drawing together the interests of diverse communities into a wider holistic vision. However, the challenge is to listen to many different publics because a universal provision is assuming that public services can be accessed by all who need them.

There are some inevitable differences in the ways in which teachers, nurses, social workers, planners and architects view the public interest, which are determined by the type of public service. As students, patients or clients, there are some differences in how the public interest might be viewed because of a responsibility that some public services have to look after the public interest. A social worker may be concerned with the public interest in relation to a child 'at risk'. A nurse may see the public interest in relation to how a patient, with an infectious disease, might impact on the public interest. Safeguarding the public interest may be looking after the interests of a community so that they can have access to public services. The democratic professional has to manage these often-competing interests.

The effect of public sector reforms over the last thirty years has been to expand the influence of the private sector with the resulting retreat of the public sphere. This can be seen in several settings, for example, what was previously public space in housing development is often private space which limits public actions such as demonstrations. The privatisation of social care services has resulted in the time that a social care worker is allowed to spend with clients being limited to short periods, not enough to provide high quality care. There is a growing body of evidence to show that many public services provided by private interests operate for the benefit of their shareholders and not to address the public interest at all. The events leading to the financial collapse of Carillion shows how directors were more interested in maintaining their pay and benefits than any consideration of the public interest (Lethbridge, 2018).

What is emerging in this discussion of public interest is that there is a public interest – often called public protection – which is trying to address what is perceived as the needs of the wider public, but there are other publics which are often invisible. It is these invisible publics which the democratic professional should be trying to engage with. Effective multi-disciplinary working will depend on an awareness of a common public interest as well as the interests of different publics, for example, social care. The role of the democratic professional is to identify and work towards public services that address the needs of excluded groups.

An example of a very different way of looking at the public interest and democratic processes has been developed by architects, landscape architects, geographers and planners. This is based on a belief in the relationship between people and the land which can stimulate a capacity for action and change. This is an area where there is often a language gap between experts and citizens, but increasingly public spaces have become the focus of democratic engagement as a reaction to the privatisation of public spaces, which has crept through new housing and retail developments (Wall and Waterman, 2018). Gert Biesta (2012) also argues that the concept of the public sphere has to be connected to public space, but he links this to Arendt's belief in the interrelationship of action, freedom and plurality (Arendt, 1958: 175; Biesta, 2012: 689). If plurality is reduced, then the quality and scope of public spaces and the public sphere are limited.

If public services are delivered in the public sphere, as opposed to a public sphere which has been reconstituted as a market, to what extent can they be characterised as creating freedom for the service users? Schools and other educational institutions can provide some forms of freedom, but these may be limited by the introduction of a national curriculum, testing, league tables and other forms of monitoring. In healthcare, the concept of freedom is more difficult to identify. Ideally, care and treatment can form a type of freedom from illness and medical conditions but healthcare systems at a micro-level, for example, hospital systems, are not always conducive to creating a sense of freedom. Public planning, architecture and landscape architecture show that a sense of freedom can be incorporated into buildings and public spaces, but when space becomes privatised, this freedom will be curtailed. Social work is more difficult if seen as a form of public protection, but developmental social work can be defined as supporting communities to define and work towards their own freedoms.

This depends on understanding different parts of the public and then establishing and maintaining some form of dialogue. How to establish dialogue is one of the major challenges facing democratic professionals. Wagenaar (2007) argued for the use of philosophical hermeneutics, in which knowledge or understanding is a form of dialogue. His use of philosophical hermeneutics takes the grounding of interpretation in everyday experience (Wagenaar, 2007:319). This can be seen as a way of understanding people's life worlds. Understanding is a 'state of being'. In a public policy context this has implications for the processes of participation, collaborative and deliberative policy making (Wagenaar, 2007: 326). They are built on assumptions that interest groups within the policy process are involved in dialogue to create some form of shared meaning.

Some of the processes which are used to establish the public interest may draw on formal democratic processes that resolve, measure and build a public interest through deliberation and debate. When considering democratic processes and the role that democratic professional play in them, it is useful to look at some examples of democratic processes in the Welfare State. Although there is a growing awareness that the Welfare State did not fully incorporate democratic processes into the way it functioned, there were attempts to include some form of democratic involvement.

In the UK, Community Health Councils (CHC) were set up in 1974 to represent patients, provide opportunities for groups of local people to work on service improvements and monitor the way in which local health services were delivered. CHCs were disbanded in 2003 and replaced by a system of patient and public involvement. This new system set up local patient's forums, but with reduced resources. Local NHS trusts set up their own patient and advocacy services. Over fifteen years later, there is a reduced voice of patients and local people in the NHS. Public sector reforms, although often paying lip service to accountability issues, have not led to greater citizen involvement, but a more narrowly defined consumer role for service users.

Ranson (2018) argues that what is needed is a "foundation and formation of new forms of polity and government" (Ranson, 2018: 57), which would incorporate different ways of working with service users, delivering to users and working together to deliver together. These should all be based on a respect for a citizen's knowledge and skills and their abilities to develop them. This would form the structure and foundation of new ways of organising and delivering public services.

Manifestos

One way in which democratic professionals have started to take action in finding new ways of addressing their clients is through the creation of networks which draw up manifestos as a first step to planning action. Social workers have used conferences, networks and manifestos to draw attention to some fundamental issues facing social work and develop supportive networks of practitioners. Part of the emphasis is on returning to a values-based social work, particularly working with service users. After Jones, Ferguson, Lavalette and Penketh (Jones et al, 2004) published 'The Manifesto for Social Work and Social Justice' in 2004, a conference in 2006 "Social work: a profession worth fighting for?" led to the creation of the Social

Work Action Network (SWAN). This aims "to challenge the growing marketisation of social work and social care, and to defend a social work practice based on social justice" (SWAN, 2015). As well as campaigning, SWAN aims to reassert values within social work as a form of professional development. It works with UNISON supporting social workers on strike, care workers on strike and victimised social worker trade union members (Lavalette, 2011).

A few universities have used their prospectuses to show how higher education could be organised in a more democratic and socially just way. The Gold Paper was developed by staff and students at Goldsmiths University, London in response to the UK 2015 Green Paper on Higher Education, which set out the government's intention to privatise parts of higher education and to reduce higher education to a component of employability and economic growth. It sets out a strategy for Goldsmiths University to be "a place of learning" as defined by the people who work there and "to celebrate its creative, critical and radical ambitions". In this sense it was both restating the radical purpose and vision of Goldsmiths and making the case for a public university which is being distorted by the processes of marketization affecting higher education.

The emphasis is on everyone working in Goldsmiths to have a role in meeting the vision. The Gold Paper recommended improving systems of governance by widening of diversity and different communities (staff, students, partner institutions, businesses and professions) with new democratic structures. This is an example of how plurality can be applied to the future of higher education. A second set of recommendations included increased openness and transparency of finances as well as work on a new alternative economic model for universities which could be used to lobby the government. Recommendations for teaching included peer review, minimising casualisation of working conditions and setting up a (G)old School which would be a "space for learning and production that is open, experimental and collaborative ... fostering exchanges with artists, academics and the local community" (Gold Paper, 2016), another way of acknowledging pluralism in relation to different local communities.

There was recognition of the crucial role that central services, infrastructure and support services play in the life of the University with a recommendation to stop all outsourcing and to pay a 'living' wage. Children of all Goldsmiths' staff would be offered reduced fees and be encouraged to apply to study. The last set of recommendations supported the creation of a broad coalition with other universities to promote change in higher education policy. The process of drawing up this Gold Letter brought staff and students together to think about a vision for the future and new ways of working within a university. This approach to creating a vision allows people within an institution to think in a different and more democratic way. The process helps to make terms such as democracy more tangible.

Working with the public

One way in which these approaches to working with different publics can be put into practice is to examine some of the models of public professional and service user that have been researched in the past. The concept of "street level bureaucrats" is one model which has had an influence on understanding how public professionals and clients interact, highlighting the use of discretion by professionals. Lipsky (1980) defined "street level bureaucrats" as "public service workers who interact directly with citizens in the course of their jobs and who have substantial discretion in the execution of their work", for example, social workers, youth workers (Lipsky, 1980: 3). The initial study looked at how police, teachers, and social workers interacted with clients. Lipsky called these groups "street level bureaucrats." In this case, the way in which the discretion is used has relevance for the way in which democratic professionals can contribute to defining the public interest although there is no obvious gender analysis involved.

These front line professionals, who were pressurised by the numbers and complexity of their clients, developed ways of coping with the demand for services. Lipsky argued that their coping strategies involved creating routines and ways of simplifying the services provided for their clients, which both influenced the quality of services delivered. This view contributed to understanding how public policies are implemented through these public services. Although the overall public policy was driven from the federal government, implementation was dependent on the individual agency responsible for delivering front line services, the "street level bureaucrats". Lipsky argued that the decisions that front line workers make in response to their clients becomes the public policy. A high degree of public service commitment is characteristic of these "street level bureaucrats", although the reality of working in these services means that ideals have to be tempered by the limitations of delivering the public services.

One of Lipsky's most controversial conclusions was the "myth of advocacy", where professionals try and secure the best outcomes for their clients, which is seen as part of the professionalism of these "street level bureaucrats" (Lipsky, 1980: 72). The pursuit of altruism is incorporated into professional training. Parsons (1939) had identified altruism as one of the characteristics of professionals operating in bureaucracies. Lipsky challenged this by arguing that front line professionals were too limited by the structure of their work and their relations with clients to be effective advocates. Advocacy requires time, and this can be limited by large caseloads as well as by the ways in which organisations function, especially in times of budget cuts and limited resources. Other reasons lay in methods of assessment of clients and the effectiveness of interdisciplinary working, where the judgements are viewed not just by their own professional peers but professionals from other services and disciplines.

Lipsky argued that when "street level bureaucrats" are unable to provide the services that they feel their clients need, they deal with this by rationalising their clients in terms of backgrounds and environmental context and extent of social responsibility and structural factors. This can affect the relationship between street level bureaucrat and client. As a way of addressing the future of public services, Lipsky set out reasons why increased client autonomy resulting in influence over policy would benefit public services. Another approach would be to redefine the relationship between clients and public sector workers, making it a more democratic exchange. This might involve helping clients to understand the structures of public services and supporting them to articulate their demands and communicating. "Street level bureaucrats" could also be made more accountable to clients, by making information available about measures taken. These suggestions, made by Lipsky in 1980, can be seen as forms of democratic professionalism.

Although the analysis of "street level bureaucrats" is an insightful one, Lipsky drew some negative conclusions. He was dismissive of the discretion of "street level bureaucrats", because he saw it leading to unfair and unequal treatment of clients (Lipsky, 1980, 197). The overall effect of discretion was influenced by how well services cooperate and interact. Decisions about social services were often influenced by social security and income decisions. However, Lipsky also argued for flexibility for "street level bureaucrats", which relates back to the position of professionals within a bureaucracy. In the case of the Welfare State in Europe, "social service professionals" took on roles of promoting social rights through their work with clients, for example, case conferences with clients.

The concept of "street level bureaucrat" has influenced recent research on how professionals use discretion in their relationships with clients. Research is beginning to contribute to a critique of marketisation and privatisation of public services by focusing on "street level bureaucracies", which are hierarchical organizations in which substantial discretion lies with the line agents at the base of the hierarchy (Piore, 2011: 146). They have some of the characteristics of a bureaucracy, but have more access to discretion rather than rules and procedures. Piore (2011) drew from a literature on labour inspection that has analysed the type of decisions made by labour inspectors, who exercise discretion in a framework of tacit rules and procedures, working closely with colleagues and bound by an organisational culture. They drew on tacit knowledge as much as explicit technical knowledge (Piore, 2011). This is a challenge to the rational-choice model of public sector behaviour, which only attributes self-interest to public sector workers.

Bartels (2012) stressed the importance of public encounters or "relational, situated performances" (Bartels, 2012: 476), defined as the interaction between the state and the citizen, which has become the focus of research in public administration since the

1970s. He argued that, although there has been growing interest in how professionals interact with the public, it often focuses on the encounter in a negative sense, about how professionals and institutions inhibit their interaction with a citizen. He suggested that, instead, a meeting between citizen and public professional should be seen as a process of constant exchange and interaction. It is a "multifaceted process of interwoven situated performances which enables or disadvantages the actual abilities of public professionals and citizens to make claims, influence decisions and understand each other" (Bartels, 2012: 476). By understanding the communications which take place in these encounters, this will lead to a better understanding of the added value of these exchanges.

A public encounter is a way of "doing and being together" because public professionals and citizens exist in relationship to each other, although this relationship changes in response to the changing role of the state. More needs to be understood about how they communicate about problems, differences and conflicts. Public encounters are about communicating with people from different backgrounds, who think and communicate in different ways. Whether their public encounters are constructive will determine how they resolve conflicts and differences. More needs to be better understood and appreciated about how public professionals and citizens approach and talk to each other and some of the results of their meetings and the context within which they meet. Communicative practices should be taken seriously and will determine whether the public encounters between public professional and citizen can effectively deal with the problems that face each other (Bartels, 2012). There are important gender and race dimensions which seem to be missing in this focus on face-to-face encounters and would need to be addressed. Do women and men communicate in different ways with their clients, students and patients? Do people from Black and Minority Ethnic communities communicate in more meaningful ways with their clients, students and patients? The work of Bartels is useful in thinking about how democratic professionals can communicate with services users and citizens but there has also to be a stronger motivation to understand different service users.

Listening and sharing knowledge not just exchanging information

Democratic professionals need to have an ability to listen, help and empower as well as a commitment to work towards greater equality and mutual understanding. This element will also require the development of new relationships between professionals and service users. For example, the relationship between nurses and patients' associations has become more respectful but patients are often still institutionalised. A nurse reported that a patient can "change from being an independent person and move into hospital where they are told when to get up, eat and go to bed. This will have to change." She viewed democratic professionalism as something that exists in small pockets of the NHS, for example, relationships between nurses and patients receiving cancer treatment. Although there are now attempts to link staffing levels with the quality of patient care the system is not yet "at tipping point" towards a new set of professional nurse-patient relationships (Lethbridge, 2015).

Many of the best doctors and nurses have moved away from the old macho model of "trust me I'm a ..." Co-production involves the patient playing a part in their care but "in hospitals it is more difficult to work for co-production. Sharing access to medical records is a beginning." (Lethbridge, 2015: 267). Other developments might include having joint discussions about the right to a second opinion, with nurses explaining how a patient might complain if they are unhappy with the process.

> More professionals should share knowledge rather than hiding behind it, e.g. whether to keep a patient alive ... Being more democratic makes people more radical and this has been forced into public health which has to consider discharge arrangements, having to ask what is the home situation and so focus less on fixing problems and moving into prevention. (Lethbridge, 2015: 268)

This also shows that one approach can have multiple effects on not just the patients and service users but on the surrounding community. It is how these links are made between service users and their communities that lies at the heart of democratic professionalism. A focus on the labour dimension of Arendt's *vita activa* can help to show relationships in different ways.

Stevenson and Gilliland (2015) defined teaching as a process of social transformation which should be underpinned by values of social justice and democracy. This involves giving validity to student views, one of the aims of the Expansive Education Network, which works towards establishing lifelong learning by acknowledging that education is more than just about passing exams. It recognises that learning opportunities occur outside the classroom and that individual intelligence is expandable rather than fixed. Expansive education defines teachers as learners who are looking for and researching better outcomes (Expansive Education Network, 2015).

As an example of how professionals show respect to children, the Reggio Emilia Network of Early Years (Italy) states that "listening is a metaphor of encounter and dialogue". Early years services are places where young and old come together. The Reggio Emilia Network believes in:

> The pedagogy of listening, the experience in Reggio tries to honour the children by listening to that expression of the human being. Perhaps the pedagogy of listening may be a pedagogy for supporting a way of living with hope that it is possible to change.
> (Rinaldi, 2004: 4)

Another example of how to listen and respect children and students was the practice of a London teacher, Chris Searle, in the 1970s who published several volumes of collections of children's writing entitled 'Stepney Words'. As Chris Searle (2017) wrote in '*Isaac and I*':

> I started taking my classes out into the street around the school with their pens and notebooks, asking them to write down what they saw: the houses, the few trees, the birds, the people who passed them by.
> (Searle, 2017: 108)

He recounted that back in the classroom "the poems came teeming out about the lives of the poets and the lives of others, particularly the old" (Searle, 2017: 110).

He used a critical pedagogy approach which "exposes and deals with the issues that shape the world in which the students have to live, helping them to make sense of it in their own terms" (Davis, 2009). This approach to teaching linked language and action. Children could write about their own worlds and "became aware of struggles within their social contexts and then were motivated to take collective cultural actions" (Cortes Camarillo, 2002: section 2).

Taking a democratic approach to respect for students is not always appreciated by school management. This approach was not valued by Stepney School and the publication of "Stepney Worlds" led to the dismissal of Chris Searle. In response, students went on strike and generated national support. Although it took two years for him to be reinstated, during that period he set up a writers' group in the basement of St George's Town Hall where the students could continue with their writing. They were joined by people of different ages from the local community. Over 15,000 copies of 'Stepney Words' were sold, and the money raised was used to fund other publications. This shows that democratic actions may result in the development of new alliances. In this case young people and older people started to work together. This reflected what had emerged in the children's poems, which often had a focus on older people. It shows how plurality is not a static process. Searle took a pluralistic approach to valuing the lives and ideas of his students, but they also adopted a pluralistic approach by observing the lives of older people who lived in their community.

Working with communities

The term community is widely used and can encompass geographical communities, ethnic communities, specific interest communities, professional communities, gendered communities and imagined communities. Community is associated with underlying values of trust, reciprocity and acceptance. Sherry Arnstein (1969) developed a ladder of citizen participation which aimed to explain the wide range of terms such as community consultation, community participation and community development. It is an example of a term which has been adopted by public sector reforms, often without a commitment to working in a democratic way. There are examples of how democratic professionals have developed collaborative working with local communities. Working with communities is an attempt to both incorporate plurality into professional practice but also to expand the public sphere by involving communities which were previously marginalised.

How professional practice can be re-thought in relation to communities can be seen in the following account of how to address the structural determinants of health in a way that creates a sense of social interdependency. The social determinants of health have informed an analysis of inequalities in health for many years. William Ventres, Shafik Dharamsi, Robert Ferrer (2016) had become aware that health care professionals often see the social determinants of health – poverty, racism, violence, housing, unemployment – as 'disembodied abstractions', rather than understanding them in ways that questioned existing social structures.

As a way of trying to connect the provision of health care to a more active awareness of economic, social, environmental and political factors that determine health, Ventres et al argue for the use of a 'social interdependency' approach among health professionals. This can be developed through a process of perception, reflection and action. It starts with a more detailed understanding of the 'realities' of health inequalities/inequities and the costs of these inequities to human dignity as well as the influence of economic and political hegemony, cultural imperialism, and other social factors. The action should be to work with the community as "active and concerned citizens of health" (Ventres et al, 2016: 85). A framework of pluralism, participation, dialogue and respectful resistance is built up to shape actions but influenced by context. This is part of "re-imaging individual health in the light of the health of the public", which is a way of defining the public interest in public health.

To achieve this 'social interdependency' approach requires health professionals to examine their own beliefs and feelings (values, anxieties, interests, intentions), learning about how historical, social and economic factors have shaped the development of healthcare professionals which has led to a focus on professional activities at the expense of seeing the reality of how people who are poor and vulnerable live. Professional activities may reproduce structures of power and negatively affect poor communities. There is a need to work in solidarity and to develop a "new ethics of care" and a new politics (Ventres et al, 2016: 86).

This is a good example of a process that healthcare workers will have to go through in rethinking their attitudes and practices if they are to be more aware of how to support marginalised communities. It results in the evolution of processes of respect for communities and enabling democratic professionals to act with integrity. This is at a time when the austerity and consolidation states are actively marginalising communities through policies which create hostile climates.

The need to understand communities can draw on the analytical framework of intersectionality which Collins and Bilge (2016) see as "an approach to understanding human life and behaviour rooted in the experiences and struggles of disenfranchised people" and secondly as "an important tool linking theory with practice that can aid in empowerment of communities and individuals" (Collins and Bilge, 2016: 36). Intersectionality as an analytical tool sets out four domains of power – interpersonal, disciplinary, cultural and structural – and explains how race, class, gender, citizenship status affect people differently. As a result, insecure employment, poor housing and ill-health have different impacts on people and communities.

Intersectionality is not just an analytical tool but a framework that "highlights the role of social institutions in shaping and solving social problems" (Collins and Bilge, 2016: 16) which can be interpreted as the role which public services can play in reducing inequalities. With the changing form of the state, the way in which public services are delivered may have a constructive influence on inequalities by facilitating social inclusion or they may further promote further inequalities, for example, reducing access to welfare benefits, limiting access to healthcare.

There are several examples of how working with local communities has formed the basis of new ways of delivering health services. In the 1980s, the community health movement in the UK, informed by the World Health Organization (WHO) 'Health for All by the Year 2000' strategy, started to work with local communities on health issues, bring them together with public professionals. One of the aims of community health development projects was to improve access to services for communities whose specific needs were not well addressed by the NHS. Some of the initiatives for women's health and Black and Minority Ethnic (BME) community health led to changes in the way in which maternity services were delivered and the setting up of well-women clinics and multi-advocacy projects. Nurses were involved in some of these initiatives.

For example, Elizabeth Anionwu, when a nurse at the Central Middlesex Hospital, was involved in setting up the Brent Sickle Cell and Thalassemia Centre, a service for people with sickle cell or thalassemia. Although it was part of the NHS, the centre had formed very close links with the local black community and was sensitive to their needs. This had been achieved through networking between volunteers, patients and health professionals (Fieldgrass, 1992: 83). This type of centre was replicated in many other health districts.

Well-women clinics were another example of how a more holistic approach to health and a more democratic approach to service users resulted in a service which addressed the overall health needs of women rather than a series of specific conditions. Islington Trades Council, the National Abortion Campaign and Islington Community Health Council worked together to form five Well-Women clinics in Islington Health Centres (Dale and Foster, 2012). For nurses working in Well-Women clinics, a change in practice was required which changed their relationship with the services users, who were not necessarily ill. Women most often visited a Well-Women clinic with questions about their reproductive health, which might be to do with controlling their fertility or having preventive tests, e.g. smear tests.

Community health development projects were part of a movement in the late 1980s which drew professionals and communities together. Women played a dominant role in creating and developing these projects. For many women from local communities, the experience of becoming part of a community development project led to education and training which transformed their lives. Many of the public professionals who worked with these projects were also women. The development of the women's health movement which started in the United States but also took root in the UK was another example of how working as part of a community on women's health issues started to challenge conventional professional attitudes towards women's health and how women were treated.

Another way of working with communities is by examining the relationship between the makeup of the workforce and those receiving public services. Diverse workforces are more sensitive to the needs of the local community. A trade unionist gave an example:

> In a health care context, if the workforce does not reflect the local community then it will not reflect the health needs of the local population. For example, how does a white dermatologist see black skin problems? (Lethbridge, 2015: 231)

Democratic institutions delivering public services will require policies which support their recognition and integration into local communities in specific ways. Roger Klein (2014) in his report for NHS England entitled 'Snowy White Peaks' examined how the more senior levels of the NHS still do not reflect the communities which it works with, even though in many cities, the majority of NHS staff are from Black and Minority Ethnic communities. This is despite over ten years of action to improve race equality.

The importance of making connections between schools, colleges and communities was recognised in more specific community education projects. The Cockpit Arts Centre in London, between 1979 and 1985, provided an example of a community-based project which ran a mix of out-of-school, after-school and holiday projects for young people and used photography as a form of creative expression. The approach taken by the project was informed by youth and community arts projects where arts workers had developed open and informal ways of working, with bases in working class communities (Dewdney and Lister, 1988: 4). Dewdney and Lister argued that in arts education, recognition of the cultural productivity of young people should be central. The Cockpit Arts Project was a progressive way of encouraging young people to reflect on their lives as well as helping young people to acquire new skills (Sefton-Green, 2013). It is the process of facilitating and training that makes this democratic because it demonstrates openness to the lives of young people and providing ways of enabling them to express the nature of their lives through photography.

Thinking differently

This section outlines several examples of how democratic professionals have started to develop different relationships with public service users. There are various triggers that can lead to a more democratic action. An external event or a perceived need which required support from several groups of stakeholders was the most frequent trigger, but individual experiences can also result in new forms of practice. Working to strength the public sphere can take many forms, but it depends on a strong sense of how to promote plurality. Women took on leadership roles in some of these examples.

Croxteth School

A comprehensive school in Liverpool, Croxteth Comprehensive, was threatened with closure by Liverpool Education Committee in the early 1980s. Parents occupied the school and a three-year occupation between December 1980 and July 1983 kept the school open (Stephen King Photography, 2013). This campaign was significant in that it brought together parents, teachers and local activists in a different relationship to that of a conventional school.

All three groups had to work out their different views of discipline, curriculum and school organisation (Carspecken III, 1987). The three-year experience highlighted some of the wider issues raised when teachers and other stakeholders work together, which were often not easy to resolve. Trade unions became involved in the campaign later in the process, although members of the campaign had close links with the Labour Party and trade unions. There were differences between the parents, teachers and students. Although the school was occupied, the education taking place in the classrooms still followed a conventional curriculum and so the students did not feel any sense of solidarity (Carspecken III, 1987). Time constraints, numbers of teachers and existing resources were some of the reasons why in the first few weeks of the occupation more had not been done to establish a more progressive curriculum.

The occupation of Croxteth Comprehensive took place over three years and showed some of the issues, in the longer term, raised by different stakeholders working together to keep a school open. It took place in Liverpool which had a distinctive local politics. Alliances changed over the three-year period. Teachers were unable to develop a progressive curriculum due to lack of resources.

There were conflicts between teachers and community teachers about the proper role of the teacher. Discipline was another source of conflict between teachers and parents. The occupation came to an end when Labour gained control of the City Council and announced that the school would remain open in 1985, three years after the occupation started.

Gender dynamics had a strong influence on the occupation. Of the teachers who volunteered for varying lengths of time, the majority were men and the ratio of men to women teachers increased over the three years. Many women teacher volunteers left because of sexist attitudes by other teachers and the community. This was in contrast to the volunteer teachers from the local community, who were mainly women (Carspecken III, 1987: 309).

Dismantling the Master's House

Another more recent example of where education is being approached in a more pluralist way can be seen in the campaign 'Dismantling the Master's House', which is based at University College London. It is part of a much wider global campaign to challenge what are increasingly seen as predominantly white-dominated academic disciplines. In 2014, the National Union of Students published the results of research into the presence of Black and Minority Ethnic groups in academia in the United Kingdom. The research found that of 18,550 professors only 85 are racialised as black and only 17 racialized and gendered as black women. This inequality is also reflected in the curriculum. What are considered as classic academic texts are dominated by white, Anglo-centric assumptions. This is reflected in the low-representation of Black and Minority Ethnic groups in the university hierarchy. However, the percentage of students racialized as black is 6% which is higher than the 3% in the population, but lower than the percentage in London which is 11.2%.

The campaign included a public lecture 'Why isn't my Professor Black?', where a panel of academics reflected on the question. Professor Shirley Anne Tate encouraged her audience to "envision conditions under which our Professors could be Black, moreover Black women" (Runnymede Trust, 2014).

The campaign has encouraged the analysis of historical figures, for example, Francis Galton and his role in the study of eugenics which has had such an influence on biology and public policies in many countries. The 'Dismantling the Master's House' campaign aims to question the legacies of the Empire in the UK and internationally and to "formulate a new radical and critical way of producing and consuming knowledge about race and to challenge the unjust racialized hierarchies which still dominate" (Dismantling the Master's House, 2018). This is a campaign, started by a group of activists within universities who have made their own institutions aware of the racialised hierarchies of higher education and the impact that this has on knowledge creation. It has started to raise awareness within higher education.

New settings for social work

Social workers are already learning from other settings about how professionals deliver services and this process is beginning to make social workers review their own ways of working, making them more aware of their own values and fallibilities.

Lawyers are involved in courts in different ways so social workers began to realise that they can have different 'voices' and roles within this system, which enable them to contribute their legal expertise as well as individual experience. To achieve this requires extensive rethinking of the social worker professional identity, basing the changes on learning from other professions about how to do things differently...

There is a sense of unity and strength in saying, 'this is a group of people who I want to be identified with' and... professional identity is important and so proactive in working together. (Lethbridge, 2015: 269)

How this is put into practice is illustrated by the following example of social workers who have changed their professional practice to enable them to work with asylum seekers more effectively.

Social workers have responded to the needs of asylum seekers in ways that show how a democratic professionalism can develop when the needs of a marginalised community are not being met. This shows how extending the public sphere to include groups previously excluded is part of the practice of a democratic professional. The preparation and training of social workers to meet the needs of asylum seekers in Liverpool led to changes in social work practice through the writing of a handbook entitled "*Good Practice of Promoting Multi-Disciplinary Working with Asylum Seekers and Refugees – The Social Work Perspective*" (Lilo et al, 2015). This raises wider questions about how to educate public professionals to be democratic professionals.

Liverpool is a member of the City of Sanctuary network of towns and cities which works towards making urban centres more welcoming and supportive to refugees and migrants. Social workers, particularly social work students, working with Asylum Aid and the Merseyside NHS Trust found that the provision of information was central to working effectively with refugees but that social workers did not necessarily either possess this information or have immediate access to it.

The handbook was written from a student perspective over a ten-year period, reflecting the period that local agencies have worked together. It was supported by Lecturers/Practice Educators at the Liverpool John Moores University, Liverpool Hope University, the Mersey Care NHS Trust, social work students and the Asylum Link Merseyside (ALM) Complex Needs Caseworker. By 2015, the fifth edition of the handbook reflected the most up-to-date information about refugee rights and services.

Trainee social workers are made aware, through their work at Asylum Aid, of the way in which the Home Office treats refugees and the difficulties in securing basic needs, such as food, housing, income, education, reducing social isolation and boredom as well as dealing with "No recourse to public funding" when their claims are rejected. The handbook provides information about legislation, rights and benefits but integrates this with discussions of a range of theories which are illustrated with specific examples. The handbook is a good example of how information can help a social worker in training to access a knowledge base which is new, but will enable them to develop their practice to respond to the needs of a group which is highly marginalised and discriminated against. Part of the process is learning to respect and act with integrity. An important part of this process is effective inter-agency working. Asylum Aid, in working with statutory agencies and universities, has played a lead role in raising awareness of how to support refugees.

The core of acting democratically is an openness to listen and involve people from groups experiencing discrimination and racism. Creating a handbook to help other social workers is expressing professional integrity by questioning how social workers can help refugees and recognising that more information and training is needed. This brings into question the existing knowledge base of social workers by finding ways of making it more relevant and better able to meet the needs of their clients.

Solutions to unmet needs

With the expansion of professional networks, the opportunities for developing new approaches drawing from different national experiences are becoming an accepted part of professional development. With the extension of austerity policies and public sector reforms, international solidarity is one way of exchanging ideas about new ways of delivering public services. The goals of pursuing a pluralist approach and expanding and making the public sphere inclusive are not necessarily limited to national boundaries.

Social Workers without Borders

Social workers have already been working with refugees and migrants in different cities in the UK for several years. The development of a training manual in Liverpool for social workers was created as a response by trainee social workers to a lack of information. It was supported by several agencies, including Asylum Aid, as outlined earlier in this chapter. Another response by social workers to the problems faced by young asylum seekers resulted in the creation of a new organisation 'Social workers without borders' to work with asylum seekers and refugees in Calais. This is an example of how democratic professionals, two women social workers, responded to a crisis in the provision of support for refugees, particularly the safeguarding of children, which the UK government has failed to address by refusing to allow more children to be admitted to the UK as asylum seekers (The Guardian, 2016).

Social workers in many countries are working with asylum seekers, refugees and migrants as part of statutory and voluntary services. Some countries have been more responsive and welcoming to recent migrants, but other countries have created a hostile environment. A specific emergency was identified by a group of UK social workers in 2016 in relation to unaccompanied children who had travelled to Europe but were and are at risk of abuse and exploitation. Although Interpol reported that 10,000 unaccompanied asylum seeking/migrant children have disappeared since entering Europe, there has not been a coordinated social work response (King and Grant, 2016).

In February 2016 two social workers from Kent set up 'Social Work First' as a response to the safeguarding issues found in the Calais refugee camp. Children are at high risk of sexual exploitation. Over 200 volunteers worked with the 'Refugee Youth Service' and 'Women and Children's Service' in the camp during 2016. Refugee Youth Service works in France, Italy and Greece, linking action across Europe and together with 'Social Work First' identifies unaccompanied children and makes assessments which aim to strengthen their legal cases for entry into the UK, by documenting the conditions within the camp and their impact on children. These assessments could inform the continuation of care when children arrive in the UK (The Guardian, 2016).

Social Work First recognises that there is a need for action at a social and political level. As well as using their expertise to assess children, in their professional role social workers are also lobbying both the French and UK governments to change public policies which demonise and exclude migrants in order to recognise their human rights. Working effectively in the Calais camp involved collaboration with other organisations and now Social Work First has merged with Social Workers without Borders (SSWB). The expanded SSWB is now working with the Social Work Action Network and the British Association of Social Workers to develop a strategy of social work action in solidarity with refugees and migrants. SSWB states "We believe that our social work skills and knowledge can be utilised to minimise risk and promote the rights and dignity of those affected by borders" (King and Grant, 2016). It was set up as a reaction to the hostility, racism and lack of care and compassion shown to refugees and migrants.

Conclusion

Several of these examples and case studies have shown how democratic professionalism has resulted in an expansion of the public sphere for groups which were previously either invisible or excluded. Children in Stepney through their writing entered a new public sphere which they later were able to develop with other older people in the community.

Community-based ways of working were much more widely used in the 1970s and 1980s. Community projects and initiatives were often subject to extensive changes, which were sometimes positive in the sense that services were taken on by mainstream providers. However, they were also subject to changes in the groups leading the activities or changes in the organisation and funding of the statutory services which provided funding and resources that supported them, for example, many youth work initiatives stopped when the Inner London Education Authority was disbanded. This shows that democratic professionalism is a dynamic process that changes over time and not always in a positive way. This is particularly relevant at the current time.

Working with other organisations and agencies can provide more opportunities to develop services which are more democratic and meet different needs though sharing expertise and resources. Service users and other stakeholders may sometimes initiate the changes, but democratic professionals have to evolve a way of working collectively with a wide range of groups.

Social workers have responded to more recent crises in the provision of services for refugees and migrants, which are' not being addressed by statutory agencies. Democratic professionals are working in a way in which expertise can be shared and built up collectively. How new organisations which have been set up will be integrated into the public sector in future is one of the biggest challenges facing democratic professionals.

In the next chapter, there will be a more specific focus on what makes democratic professionals take action. It explores the context of some of their actions and how they have resulted in new ways of delivering public services. This has been accompanied by new organisations and new ways of using professional experience in a more democratic way.

5

How to take action?

Chapters 3 (Identifying diverse forms of expertise) and 4 (Developing an inclusive public sphere) examined ways in which democratic professionals have used the search for greater plurality and the expansion of the public sphere as strategies to work more democratically. As has been shown, plurality and strengthening the public sphere complement and inform each other.

This chapter will explore the concept of responsibility within democratic professionalism, which involves accepting that there are dilemmas inherent in professional work and that relationships between professional–student, professional–client and professional–patient are increasingly difficult to resolve. Responsibility is part of the motivation to take action, but will emerge from many of the processes discussed in relation to expertise, respect and integrity. The way in which a sense of responsibility is translated into identifying opportunities to work democratically will depend on recognising the existing limitations of professional practice. How democratic professionals address responsibility will depend on a combination of agency and voice, which will enable them to break out of their existing ways of working. For example, teachers will have to exercise professional agency in both an individual way as well as by taking collective action (Stevenson and Gilliland, 2015: 6).

Hannah Arendt's concept of natality, defined as "the new beginning inherent in birth can make itself felt in the world only because the newcomer possesses the capacity of beginning something anew, that is, of acting" (Arendt, 1957: 9), provides a useful way of understanding how democratic professionals can start to take action. Natality is part of a new way of doing things. A belief in new beginnings and change can inform the action necessary to create these changes. Birth is the capacity for action, and also the source of the capacity for action. "Natality as the constant arrival of newcomers underlies the continuing existence of the realm of politics" (Totschnig, 2017).

Just as natality can be seen as the foundation for politics, a belief in the value of action has to be the foundation of any change that democratic professionals work towards. If this approach is applied to the process of making public services more democratic and better at addressing social justice, then the first step is for democratic professionals to play a more active role within different institutions and organisations. In addition, they will have to identify potential alliances within and outside public services. In order to better understand how to take action, the concept of agency and a theory of creativity of action (Joas, 1996) will be discussed to show some of the conditions, struggles and processes that inform how people decide to take action.

Agency

The concept of agency is considered fundamental to a democratic professional taking responsibility for action. In this sense the belief in natality is expressed through agency. The sense of agency which democratic professionals will be able to exercise will depend on how they see themselves in relation to the institutions within which they work and those outside. Another way of looking at this democratic professional–institution relationship is to think about how their working environment supports innovation and agency. Public services are dependent on innovation and the contribution of public professionals to maintaining quality services depend on these professionals having a sense of their own agency, in an individual and collective sense. The impact of public service reforms has made this a much more difficult process for many public professionals. Managerialism and marketization have often made public professionals feel devalued, reduced to 'performativity' and following processes and procedures. This makes it even more important to understand what influences professional agency.

Institutional agency has to be considered in terms of gender and race relations. As mentioned in Chapter 1, there is extensive research that shows that women are often not valued within organisations, even when they are in a majority (Davies, 1994; Calás and Smircich, 1996; Wacjman, 1998; Calás and Smircich, 2006). This has implications for looking at how women as democratic professionals take action. Their position within an institution will affect how they take action. Similarly, even after several decades of race equality strategies, the representation of Black and Minority Ethnic groups within public institutions is limited and shows how their expertise and experiences are still not valued.

There has also been extensive research into the concept of agency. A useful review of research into agency was made by Emirbayer and Mische (1998) who felt that agency remained an "elusive' concept because it is so often linked to structure, for example, structuration theory (Giddens, 1979). In order to better understand the role of agency in social change, their review analysed the different ways in which agency has been interpreted as well as the varied forms of agency. The results of this review led to a re-conceptualisation of agency as the "temporal nature of human experience – past, present and future" and to imagine a future different from the past. It concluded that people are sometimes more focused on the past or the present or the future and that a sense of time has a powerful influence on how people view their own agency. Public services have their own histories intertwined with those of the public professionals that work in them.

One conclusion for democratic professionalism is that norms and values are "bi-products of actors' engagement with one another in ambiguous and challenging circumstance" (Emirbayer and Mische, 1998: 1012). They emerge when individuals face moral or practical problems and are only resolved "when actors reconstruct temporal–relational contexts and in the process, transform their own values and themselves" (Emirbayer and Mische, 1998: 1013). This is very relevant for democratic professionals when they are facing challenges from a strong management, target-driven agenda, but would like to exercise their professional judgement. It is also a way of understanding what drives democratic professionals to take action.

The contribution that Hans Joas made with his theory of 'creativity of action' helps to build on this re-conceptualisation of agency in a temporal sense (Joas, 1996). He saw that action has creativity as its centre, whether in rational or collective action. He defined action as "a common feature which is displayed whenever an actor finds a solution to a problem in a specific situation" (Weik, 2012: 571).

One problem in understanding professional agency is whether professionals can change their own institutions when their interests and values have been shaped by those same institutions (Joas, 1996; Weik, 2012: 568). This links to the view of institutional development and change (Emirbayer and Mische, 1998: 993), which highlighted that habit and routine play a role in decision-making in institutions (Powell and DiMaggio, 1991). Democratic professionals will be influenced by the institutions delivering public services. Joas's concept of corporeality examines how individuals and people working together make decisions and take action (Joas, 1996: 161). To think and act in ways that may change these institutions will require the creation of new alliances and coalitions both internally within an institution and outside it.

Joas treats the emotional experience of people within an institution in a different way to that of the conventional rational actor (Joas, 1996: 146-7). He takes a collective view, defined as when an institution can enable people to "go beyond themselves". In public institutions this can be described as the 'public ethos' which makes the sensitive delivery of public services heavily dependent on whether this 'public ethos' is nurtured and cultivated. The NHS is an example of the emotional force of an institution because it operates with a 'public ethos' which affects patients and healthcare professionals.

Joas acknowledges that agency is a product of people's imagination (Joas, 1996: 163) which may change over time according to circumstances and greater knowledge and expertise. This acknowledges the temporal dimension of agency. As people increase their understanding this may contribute to a critique of existing institutions. This is part of a hermeneutical model where an individual gradually develops an understanding of an issue while evolving a way of responding to a problem and creating action (Joas, 1996: 148). This may involve people and agencies interacting, which is also part of the hermeneutical exchange. Consequently, an individual's plans change as their understanding of an issue grows. This has parallels with Wagenaar's view of democratic dialogue, based on the use of philosophical hermeneutics, in which knowledge or understanding is a form of dialogue (Wagenaar, 2007: 326).

Building on these understandings of the historical process of agency, Eteläpelto et al (2013) reviewed the multi-disciplinary nature of agency and identified seven elements of professional agency. This provides an example of how a more temporal approach can be applied to democratic professionalism. Eteläpelto et al placed professional agency within the actions of professionals and/or communities when they exert influence, make choices, and take stances in ways that affect their work and/or their professional identities. It is exercised "within certain (historically formed) socio-cultural and material circumstances, and it is constrained and resourced by these circumstances" (Eteläpelto et al, 2013: 62).

Professional agency is strongly related to work-related identities which include professional and ethical commitments, ideals, motivations, interests and goals. These have been influenced by professional experiences, knowledge and expertise which provide opportunities for exercising professional agency at work. Professional agency is constructed within the conditions of work and is central to professional work, to working with communities and taking creative initiatives, although it is increasingly restricted. It is important for professional learning and for changing work identities and practice (Eteläpelto et al, 2013: 63). This understanding of how professional agency operates at many different levels and in different settings helps to understand the opportunities which democratic professionals have when working in public services. Understanding these processes will help to make decisions about action necessary to make public services more democratic.

Women teachers in Brazil

The importance of history and past experience is reflected in a study of women teachers who contributed to radical democratic school reforms in Brazil. After the fall of the military government in the early 1980s and the creation of a new Constitution in 1988, new democratic educational systems were created with the support of teachers' unions and state structures. Two major changes which showed how democratic changes can be introduced into public services involved the drawing together of different stakeholder groups. School administrators were elected by students, parents, staff and teachers. Community-based management arrangements, called *colegiados*, set up with representatives of teachers, parents, students and administrators were responsible for all administrative and financial decisions (Jennings and Da Matta, 2009).

Yet, the most interesting findings from the Jennings and Da Matta study is how women teachers drew on their experience of resistance during the military regime, when they were girls and young women, to shape their approach to teaching in the newly democratic school system. For some teachers their resistance was their active membership of large social and political movements, but for others it was defined by locally based actions. These experiences influenced their approach to working within the new school structures. One teacher had been introduced to Paulo Freire's liberation pedagogy when she was growing up and she used this experience when teaching her own students. She took a group to the capital, Brasilia, when the 1988 Constitution was being drafted, where her students offered their own proposals to legislators. The new democratic processes supported this teacher in her new work (Jennings and Da Matta, 2009).

Another teacher found that, although she participated in a women's consciousness raising group, she remained more conventional in her actual teaching. It was only after further study and the creation of inter-disciplinary teams in her school that she began to see herself as an educator rather than a traditional maths teacher. In both these cases, previous experiences of radical action, informed a sense of professional agency even though some form of professional support was also valued (Jennings and Da Matta, 2009).

In the UK, Hoggett, Mayo and Miller (2006) explored how the motivations of a group of public service workers, involved in regeneration projects, were influenced by their own background and experience. Their values influenced the way in which these public service workers functioned within their work environment. This provides a different perspective to that of a conventional professional identity in that it draws on the individual values and life experiences of professionals, which are not shaped so strongly by a professional training or sense of professional autonomy. It draws on the concept that there are different types of knowledge that can inform professional practice, which contributes to a stronger sense of plurality.

Stakeholder democracy

If democratic professionals are to build on the power of their own agency, they will have to be able to identify stakeholders who should be involved in future action. Stakeholder theory was originally developed in the corporate sector and aimed to explain the relationships between companies and key interest groups, e.g. shareholders, employers, government, trade unions. If it is considered in the context of stakeholder democracy, it is a useful way of starting to think about which institutions democratic professionals should engage with. Stakeholder analysis is a process that already happens in many specialist services and can be applied to wider service delivery, including public services. It supports the view of Dewey, who believed that "all those who are affected by social institutions must have a share in producing and managing them" (Dewey, 1987: 218). This is an important concept to inform the development of democratic professionalism.

Matten and Crance (2005) use the term 'stakeholder democracy' to describe this process. They argue that stakeholders should be invited to participate in strategic decision-making when their well-being and rights are affected. Shareholder democracy in a private sector context is defined as the participation of shareholders in the organizing, decision-making and governance of corporations and in public institutions could include citizens taking on these roles. The concept of stake can be defined in different ways, including 'interest' and 'voice' (Fassin et al, 2017).

Research into the not-for-profit sector, which often uses a model of stakeholder democracy to involve service users in the management and evaluation of services has found that there are similarities in stakeholder management and participative management. Fassin et al (2017) in a study of youth guidance homes in Belgium, where young people were the major stakeholders, found that young people and their parents valued being able to contribute to operational management more than to strategic management. They also identified a large number of external stakeholders whose roles changed over time. A funder might cease to exist, and organisations may change roles when regulations require.

One of the challenges facing youth guidance homes is that young people are required to attend, but their active participation in the running of the homes is essential for success. These, sometimes contradictory, processes are common to several public services. This is a non-profit view of stakeholder theory which separates operational management and participative management from strategic management with implications for stakeholder management in public services. Whilst it recognises a reality of existing organisations, it should highlight the need to support and prepare service users in how to take part in strategic management, because this will enable them to play a stronger role in the development of a public service.

From agency to action

A democratic professional accepts that there are dilemmas inherent in professional work and that relationships between professional–student, professional–client and professional–patient are increasingly complex. These complexities may be related to the consumer pressures created by public management reforms, for example students becoming indebted by taking out loans and viewing their lecturers in terms of 'value for money' rather than part of a learning partnership. Medical treatments that allow for longer rates of survival but that may affect the quality of life raise difficult questions for both patients and healthcare professionals. Responsibility can be seen as a form of self-regulation. If professionals start to work in different ways with stakeholders, this will also require the creation of new forms of democratic accountability at the local level which go beyond self-regulation (Spours, 2014). These new forms of local accountability will need different working processes. For example, teachers would have to be involved in the running of the school, play a role in the wider educational system and supporting and showing solidarity with other teachers. However, if new local systems of accountability are created, then central government policies will have to change in order to complement and support them.

Whitty and Wisby (2006) argued that democratic professionalism would require teachers to take responsibility for more than just their actions in the classroom. Teachers would have to be involved in the running of the school, play a role in the wider educational system, supporting and showing solidarity with other teachers. However, teachers would also have to recognise that the solution to social problems and wider social agendas may have to involve the subordination of professional interests, perhaps one of the most important elements of democratic professionalism. This can be seen in the occupation of Croxteth School, where the interests of teachers had to be negotiated with parents, students, activist and local trade unions.

Social workers providing expert services

Within social work, providing information to people with disabilities as part of personalised care policies, which help disabled people to manage their own services, can be seen as another way of addressing competence. Personalised services provide many people with disabilities with greater freedom to organise their lives, but individual personalisation may lead to increasing fragmentation of public services. Social workers are having to rethink how they deliver their services, which involves the questioning of the knowledge and expertise that they require in different settings. They are starting to learn from other professionals about how to provide expert advice as well as how to draw in the knowledge and skills of service users.

> Social workers have been looking at how to provide expert services within family courts services, grouped together in the Children and Family Court Advisory and Support Service (CAFCAS). Social workers provide expert services and also provide expert witnesses. Courts wanted advice about how to get the best advice. (Lethbridge, 2015: 267)

A trade union respondent observed that:

> Democratic professionalism has been the focus of a significant discussion in their organisation, which has a growing membership at a time when other trade unions and professional associations are in decline. (Lethbridge, 2015: 268)

Social workers are faced with a difficult question in relation to democratic professionalism. They have responsibility for the *"protection side and also performance responsibility for protection"*, which can conflict.

> The uncertainty of the employment environment is forcing those social workers to think differently about their future because they can't rely on local government. Some social workers work in the NHS, which is challenging and they see other professionals, for example, in relation to continuous professional development, where cross-learning has helped people to think about what is done. The reforms have created a lot of debate, with some members passionate about the role of social work in local government and want to fight any reforms that destabilise that link. (Lethbridge, 2015: 269)

For social workers, the concept of democratic professionalism is providing a way of getting them to think about their future and how they want to work. Other public professionals, such as architects and planners, have started to use their professional expertise in different ways, also in response to either a crisis or demand for new ways of operating. The following examples show how the pursuit of plurality underpins any action. Architects and planners have a much more conscious awareness of the public sphere in a spatial and social sense.

The 'Gutter to Gulf' Project

An example of how landscape architects took responsibility for action can be found in New Orleans after Hurricane Katriona. Although New Orleans was originally built on the high ground of the banks of the Mississippi, in the twentieth century it expanded onto low lying swamps nearer to the river. After the devastation of Hurricane Katriona, an academic landscape architect, Jane Wolff, was working with grass roots groups and found that there was very little information available about drainage systems and the local ecology. This made it difficult to be able to plan for the future, because there was the unknown threat of further flooding. She drew together a group of landscape architects from Toronto and Washington State Universities, who identified this lack of information as a political problem which would hinder responsible design proposals and design research (Wolff, 2018: 37). Both academics and students worked with Jane Wolff to research the hydrological and hydraulic systems of New Orleans and to make the information gathered available in terms that citizens, planners, urban designers, policy makers and politicians could all understand.

Called the 'Gutter to Gulf' project, this was part of a process of bridging a knowledge and language gap between experts and citizens. It was an essential step in facilitating debate about the relationship of New Orleans to water in technical and political terms. It shows how important language is in making processes and services more democratic. Language influences decision-making with public institutions. Democratic professionals can focus on how issues are presented and work towards making them more accessible in terms of content and the different ways in which this content is expressed.

Architects for Social Housing

Set up by an architect, Geraldine Dening, Architects for Social Housing is a collective of architects, urban designers, engineers, planners, academics, theatre directors, photographers, writers and housing activists which has started to take action against the London housing crisis by providing expertise and working with residents of public housing estates at risk of redevelopment in London. The collective works with a set of principles:

1. to propose alternatives to the demolition of public housing estates through infill, build-over and refurbishment;
2. to disseminate information that aims to counter negative perceptions about social housing in the minds of the public and relevant interest groups using a variety of means, including protest; and
3. to support estate communities in their resistance to the demolition of their homes by working with residents, offering ideas and information from a reservoir of knowledge and tactics pooled from similar campaigns. (Architects for Social Housing, 2018)

ASH provides residents of public housing schemes with information that can be used to challenge local authority plans to demolish estates, to be replaced by commercial housing developments. But this action is not just about providing information, it also aims to change the perceptions of public housing estates.

An example of how ASH has supported estate communities can be seen in the Open Gardens Estates initiative. This was a series of events where public housing estates, often at risk of re-development were opened to the public in order to show the character of the community living there and their plans for the future. Tenants and Residents Association provided guided tours of their communal gardens. Kate Macintosh, the architect of Dawson's Heights, an estate that she designed in the mid-1960s, spoke at one of the Open Gardens Estates events and said, "Central to all housing design is the balance between the expression of the individual dwelling and the cohesion and integration of the entire group" (Elmer and Dening, 2015). ASH argues that the destruction of public housing estates in London is part of a process of demolishing the Welfare State. ASH thinks that architects have to defend London housing estates and to learn from their vision of the role of architecture in society, where architecture is a social model rather than financial asset.

Assemble

Other architects are beginning to address some of these issues in different ways. An architectural collective, *Assemble*, supports public involvement and partnership working as well as working with the local community, recognising its strength and resourcefulness. This approach has contributed to the regeneration of a neighbourhood (Assemble, 2015).

Assemble worked with a community in Liverpool, called Granby Four Streets, which was faced with the demolition of its houses. In 2011, the community set up the Granby Four Streets Community Land Trust (CLT), an innovative form of community land ownership, with the aim of bringing empty homes back into use as affordable housing. *Assemble* worked with the Granby Four Streets CLT and Steinbeck Studios to refurbish existing housing and public space and provide new work and enterprise opportunities.

Assemble's approach supports public involvement and partnership working as well as working with the local community, recognising their strength and resourcefulness. This approach has contributed to the regeneration of the neighbourhood (Assemble, 2015). *Assemble* set up the Granby Workshop, which sells experimental, handmade products for homes, all of which are made in the local area. Each product they sell is unique and all profits go back into the business, which trains and employs local people.

The work of both Architects for Social Housing and *Assemble* show how architects and other professionals involved in public housing have taken action to work with local communities to safeguard and develop their homes. ASH has several ways of taking action. It combines work on alternatives to regeneration with the communities affected with campaigning for a new approach to public housing in London. Their form of democratic engagement supports communities in changing the image of public housing as well as providing information to challenge local authority decision-making. *Assemble*, working on a smaller scale, has developed more democratic ways of working with residents in housing development, so that they build on the work of the local community, complementing skills and contributing to further strengthening the community. Both parts of this dual approach reflect a broader conception of action. It is not just an application of professional practice in a democratic way, but it also aims to change public policies and public attitudes.

StreetDoctors

StreetDoctors is an organisation which provides information and practical first aid skills for young people so that they can act when someone is bleeding or unconscious. Its aim is to reduce mortality and morbidity among young people. The project started when two trainee doctors were teaching first aid to young people in the Liverpool young offenders' service. They asked the group that they were teaching if anyone had seen a stabbing. Everyone in the group put their hands up. This inspired them to take action and set up StreetDoctors.

The organisation recruits medical students to give specialised first aid training to young people who are at high risk of violence, who may be young offenders or young people living in areas with high rates of youth violence. They aim to provide the young people with skills which will be useful in an emergency, but also to enable them to build up their confidence to change their attitudes towards violence. They found that young people often have "a perception that it is safe to stab someone in certain areas of the body and many young people are unaware of the potentially life-changing impacts of a non-fatal stabbing". The project tries to counter this view by explaining what the major organs do and what happens when someone loses blood (Red Quadrant/StreetDoctors, 2015: 36).

The impact of their work can be seen in several incidents where a young man has been knifed and another young man who had taken part in this specialised first aid training was able to stop the bleeding and stay with him until the ambulance arrived, so saving his life. The volunteers try and make the connection between carrying a knife and experiencing the devastating results of knife violence which can result in death or long-term disability.

StreetDoctors has now developed Stepwise, a peer education programme which is run over three to six months and aims to empower young people at risk of violence to learn, share and teach emergency lifesaving skills.

There are two steps. In Step One:

1. young person attends a StreetDoctors 'what to do when someone is bleeding' module;
2. young person attends a StreetDoctors 'what to do when someone is unconscious' module;
3. young person attends a one day accredited first aid at work course; and
4. young person attends a careers day to explore pathways into healthcare professions.

When young people have completed the training, they are given first aid accreditation and career guidance. During Step Two a young person receives training to co-facilitate sessions with medical volunteers.

This is an example of democratic professionals identifying a need and developing a different way of approaching a problem. By making a connection between the violence that young people experience and the first aid skills that the trainee doctors were teaching, they were able to provide an empowering way of supporting young people at risk of violence. The project has built in a component of supporting young people to develop new skills which may lead to following a career in healthcare.

These examples show how democratic professionals took action in response to a problem. It is interesting to see that two of the projects were set up by women, operating initially outside an institution, although ultimately working collectively with other professionals and students. All these projects show that taking action depended on an understanding of a wider environment. This can be seen in terms of expanding the public sphere.

Action through changing professional awareness

Unger (2005) argued that the future provision of public services must be an *"innovative collective practice"*, but with innovation coming from below rather than imposed from the top (Unger, 2005: 179). Democracy has to inform these new processes. This section discusses several cases where democratic professionals started to think in a different way about their responsibilities which resulted in new types of political action, not necessarily directly associated with their original public profession.

Radical Nurses Group

By the 1970s, nurses were starting to question the medical model that dominated the NHS and which nurses felt compromised the quality of care they were able to provide for patients. Underlying this concern for patient care was a more fundamental struggle between nurses and doctors, with nurses trying to challenge the rigidity of the medical model and moving towards a more holistic model of health. This shows how nurses were beginning to exercise their professional agency. They were questioning their existing professional practice and found that this was not addressing the needs of the patients, which required looking critically at existing professional relationships.

Radical Nurses Groups (RNG) were set up around 1980 in England "by and for nurses because of the dissatisfaction so many of us have about so many aspects of our jobs" (New Left Project, 2013). The newsletters produced by the Radical Nurses Group show some of the issues that nurses discussed. They show that they were attempting to articulate a new way of thinking about patient care. These examples show the problems that were faced by nurses. The adoption of a collective approach to solving the problems of professional practice showed the strength of action taken collectively.

> The lack of adequate communication between doctors and patients can be very frustrating for nurses who think that patients should be given a clear idea of what is happening to them, as the

decision to tell a patient her diagnosis rests with the consultant, even though very often the nurses will know a patient much better than the doctors do. So the patient, being treated for a fatal disease without her knowledge, because of doctors' inadequacy at communicating often comes to the realisation of impending death alone, with the reality being consistently denied by both doctors and nurses.... Thus a profession which is predominantly female continues to be intimidated by a profession which is predominantly male. Medical staff are educated within a system which sees acute medicine as having more status and power than a 'caring' speciality like geriatrics. For this reason, they come to see 'caring' as unimportant in terms of their career. A radical change in both nursing and medical education is needed to promote caring as well as curing. (MT in Radical Nurses Group (RNG) Newsletter: January 1981)

The RNG campaigned for "a distinctive 'nursing' voice". This was to be achieved in part through the "evolution of an overtly 'feminine' discourse of care, centred on compassion". The RNG used a feminist analysis to examine the role of nurses and relationships with the medical profession. At that time, nurses often argued against taking on tasks done by doctors, not wanting to dilute their caring role, although this has now changed. The RNG was an attempt to provide support for nurses who felt that questioning the power of the medical model was necessary to improve the quality of patient care. They were also questioning the nature of their own professional power.
  A contributor to the RNG Newsletter in 1988 wrote:

I think we must look closely at some of the foregone conclusions we assume as 'those with knowledge' who 'know best'. I remember asking a patient whether they would like to change their position in bed and being quite aghast at their response: "you know best, nurse. What do you think?" I explained the nature and necessity of pressure area care but asserted that it is the patient who knows most about their degree of discomfort and can best advise the caring staff on such a personal matter. This small incident made me realise what power I held and not surprisingly, made me feel quite inadequate to take on such responsibility as a student on my second ward. I wonder how much power we consider the patient has in relation to their nursing care? (DB in Radical Nurses Group (RNG) Newsletter Autumn 1988)

The importance of the Radical Nurses Group was to provide support for nurses who wanted to look at nursing and healthcare practice in a more critical way. It challenged the stereotyping of nurses and helped to make nursing recognised as a profession. More importantly the Radical Nurses Group provided the space and opportunities for nurses to challenge existing practice, to support each other and to start to think about a more radical, patient centred type of healthcare. Members of the Radical Nurses Group went on to influence policy at different levels in the NHS.

The importance of this group was to provide support for nurses who were not valued within the NHS. It is an example of how professionals who would like to become democratic professionals can meet together to provide support for each other and to advance thinking around how to improve patient care. Since then there have been gradual changes in the role and position of nurses, changes in nurse training and the introduction of an all-graduate entry to the profession. However, the power imbalance between doctors and nurses still exists and continues to affect the nature of healthcare. This should also be seen in terms of women professionals challenging existing institutional arrangements which they felt prevented them from providing patient-centred care.

National Union of Teachers and political organising

In 2014, the National Union of Teachers realised that it needed to re-new the trade union in the light of changes that had taken place in schools. Collective bargaining was no longer carried out nationally and had been devolved to individual schools or groups of schools. This placed greater responsibility on local union members who had to be able to bargain at local school level. The union also wanted to strengthen links between teachers and parents and to support them to campaign on common issues and make teaching perceived in a much more positive way. This led to the NUT creating a new organising strategy which aimed to increase member recruitment and develop wider political campaigns. The approach has drawn from the experience of Chicago teacher unions in the United States, which reached out to the community with community organising strategies.

A trade unionist said:

> The position of the NUT is that we see that we want to renew the union, organise at grass roots level and get teachers talking to parents and other teachers. There is some sign of this working, with members starting to challenge over workload and about the content and control of work. We want to move from a negative account of teaching to a more active approach as seen on Twitter, where teachers are writing, and "I've got an idea about how to teach." If the union can instil its campaigns with this sort of spirit, then it can demonstrate educational rebirth. The NUT wants to campaign like this and has moved significant resources into an organisational team......It has remodelled training for school reps, trying to get teacher voice, building collectively so that they can take issues to the Head. Action will be approached at school level. (Lethbridge, 2015: 186)

The approach also tries to address the challenges of collective bargaining, which has now been delegated down to school level, because there is no longer any national collective bargaining framework for teachers. Teachers and union members have to be supported to bargain at local school level. This approach has drawn from the experience of Chicago teacher unions in the United States, which reached out to the community.

An example of how the NUT is starting to influence the democratic process can be seen in the publication of a manifesto 'Vote for Education' to inform the 2015 election campaign. 1.6 million copies were printed. It covered issues ranging from a wider vision of learning, more time for teaching not tests, child poverty, ending the school places crisis, mending a fractured education system, ending for-profit education, investing in education, making teaching an attractive profession (NUT, 2015). This showed a teaching union taking a holistic vision of what an educational system should look like and campaigning for it during a general election campaign. An immediate result was that there is now a national parent movement which is campaigning to withdraw children from Standard Attainment Tests (SATS).

The manifesto outlined a set of issues that teachers were encouraged to raise with parents. It recommended that:

- all students should be entitled to benefit from a broad, balanced and enriching curriculum;
- a new national council for curriculum and assessment should be established to bring together teachers, employers and parents to develop an exciting vision for education; and
- a coherent 14–19 qualifications framework is needed, which unifies all learning routes, both academic and vocational. (NUT, 2015)

The Manifesto covered issues that are central to children's lives. It called for a wider demand that education should be run as a public good and not for profit. A future government should recognise that education requires investment and a return to 2010 levels of funding (NUT, 2015). The manifesto addressed the needs of children through engaging in the democratic process. This reflects the important role that trade unions can play in supporting members to be democratic professionals.

This trade union strategy is developing a new form of teacher professionalism which will focus more on addressing problems within schools through a stronger teacher 'voice'. It is contributing to rethinking the role of a teacher and making the democratic professional teacher better able to deal with issues at local level through working with parents and local stakeholders. This shows the important role that trade unions can play in supporting the development of democratic professionalism. However, this strategy has not yet been reflected in the new National Education Union (NEU) which was created from a merger of the National Union of Teachers and the Association of Teachers and Lecturers in 2017.

Schools response to Grenfell Tower fire

An example of how teachers took action when children and families were affected by a major crisis can be seen in the response of schools near to the Grenfell Tower fire in North Kensington, London.

The Grenfell Tower fire in June 2017, when 71 people died, was the highest loss of life through fire in a generation in the UK. The circumstances that led to the fire show that some public professionals in Kensington and Chelsea Council and the Kensington and Chelsea Tenant Management Organisation, the agency which had been contracted to run the housing block, had failed to listen to the concerns of the residents about fire safety in the block. Residents were an ethnically diverse community in North Kensington who were not given any voice in decisions to protect their homes. A public inquiry has been set up to examine the causes of the fire but the struggle to get people affected by the fire to be a recognised as part of the enquiry shows that a sense of democratic professionalism has not informed the response to the disaster by either central or local government.

In contrast, the response of local primary schools shows how democratic professionals took action in a time of crisis and found ways of meeting the needs of local communities affected by the fire. This was an example of how a sense of plurality and the importance of expanding the public sphere to include people affected by this disaster have informed the action of many schools. During the night of the fire, one headmaster went to the rescue centre and offered practical help in the form of new uniforms and bags for children and free places in breakfast and after-school clubs. After the fire, schools had to cope with children who had experienced family bereavements, were homeless and had to deal with the loss of friends. The schools laid on special events for these young survivors – visits to the theatre, lunch with the head teacher, hot chocolate. The head teachers attended the funerals of the children who died. Although these were specific actions, there has been a wider approach within the schools of acknowledging the grief that many families and teachers have felt. This has required a combination of an increased caring role with the need to provide a stable environment for children and families made homeless by the fire (Rustin, 2017).

The schools are located in the middle of the communities directly affected by the fire. There is a strong sense of community in social and spatial terms. Many teachers have lived in the area for many years and so are part of the community, which is unusual. As children grow up strong links are made between children, families and schools. After the fire, both children and adults have been experiencing a sense of loss which will continue for a long time.

Over five months after the fire, in her first press interview, a head teacher explained why she had not wanted to talk to the press.

> It's almost like locking the gates to keep everyone safe and so we can work through it together. Because we don't really know what we're doing and the only way we can do that is by not having anyone watching us. (Sarah Cooper quoted in Rustin, 2017)

This head teacher said that 'we don't really know what we're doing' which is admitting a professional (and personal) vulnerability but she is not doubting what the school has been doing. It is just that it is a new and unknown experience for everyone involved in the school. The school has taken on a caring and supportive role for children and the local community which has widened the scope of what a school can do. This is significant for future learning about how schools and education services can take responsibility for their children and students in a way that impacts on many aspects of their lives, their families and local communities. Many schools have taken a similarly broad view of their responsibilities in relation to child poverty.

Forensic Architecture

Another example of a profession that has expanded the use and interpretation of its professional skills can be seen in Forensic Architecture. Architects have applied their professional knowledge and expertise to wider issues than conventionally covered by one profession. This process started by one architect thinking critically about professional practice. Eyal Weizman, a British-Israeli architect, began by studying how architecture and planning were used to 'divide and suppress' people in the 'occupied territories'. He showed that there could be human rights violations by architecture and planning (Moore, 2018). His way of taking action was to apply the techniques and expertise of architecture to investigate state violence and human rights violations, in what has become known as a sub-discipline of architecture, Forensic Architecture. Eyal Weizman went on to found Forensic Architecture, a unit at Goldsmiths University, London. The underlying belief is that architects should be public figures taking public positions, whatever they do (Moore, 2018).

Forensic Architecture works with communities affected by state and police violence alongside non-governmental organisations (NGOs), as a type of 'architectural detective agency'. It uses multiple forms of evidence, for example, open-sourced citizen produced media and blogs, social media posts and state documents. The use of architectural techniques, for example the creation of physical and digital models, usually applied in the creation of buildings and other structures can show a three-dimensional version of events, using spatial and non-spatial models, which provide a theoretical understanding of the way in which an incident unfolds and predicts how an incident developed.

A recent example of the application of these techniques was an investigation into Bedouin rights in Negev. On 18 January 2017 in the village of Negev Des Umm al-Huan, a Bedouin villager and an Israeli policeman were killed. The Israeli police force had raided the illegalised Bedouin village to demolish some houses. It claimed that the incident was a '"terror attack' by Abu al-Qi'an, and further, that he had links to Daesh (ISIS)" (Forensic Architecture, 2018). Forensic Architecture was able to reconstruct the events, which supported the eyewitness version of events from local residents and activists which showed that Abu al-Qi'an had lost control of his vehicle and ran over the policeman "only after being shot by an Israeli policeman". He was left to bleed to death.

Forensic Architecture uses a technique called the 'Image data complex', which brings together images from many different actors and satellite images and creates a detailed 3D view of a location, which can show increases in the number of people, military equipment or vehicles. Forensic Architecture has been involved in the development of open source software called PATTRN, which allows people and activists to upload information and so map relations between discrete events. This is an example of how professionals are sharing expertise and enabling citizens to take part in reconstructing events that challenge accounts made by state authorities.

Another recent project, where these techniques were used was an investigation into the enforced disappearances of 43 Ayotzinapa students from rural teacher training schools in Mexico, who were on their way to a demonstration. They were attacked in Ignata, where they had travelled to change buses. Forensic architecture data-mined the reports of the violence, using reports from different sources, plotted data and built a cartographic platform to help people investigate the relations between events shared. This showed the collusion and coordinated actions of state and organised crime. A mural was created that plotted a narrative timeline of different actors, which help challenge the 'historical truth'.

One of the democratic elements of Forensic Architecture is that it provides people with access to expertise that enables them to challenge existing structures of power and control exercised by governments, police/military and organised crime. Forensic architecture has the ability to recreate events, which are not influenced by the conventional account, using techniques to map and elicit different accounts by using memory, spatial models.

This provides people with the knowledge and understanding of what happened during a specific incident. For example, Forensic Architecture is creating a free resource for the public to better understand how the fire in Grenfell Tower, London spread and what could be done to prevent a similar fire in future (Forensic Architecture, 2018a).

Conclusion

This chapter has explored how democratic professionals have taken action, sometimes within their existing settings but others have stepped away from their conventional professional roles and started to operate in a different way. The concept of agency, particularly the influence of history at an individual and institutional level can help to identify why democratic professionals have taken action. More importantly, action has to be based on a belief in the capacity of action to change things. In this sense, the belief in natality, as a way to new beginnings, is central to understanding what leads to democratic professionalism. The strategies adopted to achieve change are dependent on increasing plurality within public services and expanding the public sphere. The belief in new beginnings, plurality and a public sphere provide a strategy for taking action, originating from Arendt's search for a *vita activa*.

Several examples show how important thinking critically about existing professional practice, professional responsibilities and boundaries is in the creation of a democratic professional. Taking action can involve moving outside conventional application of professional expertise or it might require developing new ways of delivering services.

The role that women have played in these examples shows how the freedom to operate outside an institution can be a trigger for taking action. The examples of women architects, either initially working alone but often working collectively, show how action can be taken more easily outside an institution. Yet, women also take action within institutions. The Radical Nurses Group was a reaction by a profession, predominantly female, which reacted to their position and status by organising collectively and supporting a re-thinking of nursing.

What is emerging from the examples in many of these chapters is that there are two groups of democratic professional interventions, ones which work within existing service structures and those that have been set up as a separate agencies or organisations. The existence of new organisations poses questions for the future. Will this be a new public sphere? Can these be taken over and become part of the public sector? Does this undermine existing public services? Some of these questions will be discussed in the concluding chapter.

6

Conclusion

This book has argued that democratic professionalism should be the response of public professionals to the current state of public services and the changing role of the state. Democratic professionalism is an attempt to change the way in which public professionals work with service users, ultimately creating more democratic relationships. There is a long history of public professionals exploring alternative and progressive approaches to working with services users, some of which have been reviewed in this book and some of which have been taken up as mainstream practices.

However, the continued existence of many current examples of democratic professionalism is now threatened by the reduced role of the state in the provision of public services. This can be characterised as the hollowing out through outsourcing, privatisation, extensive restructuring and continued austerity policies. Increasingly the impact of these processes is leading to a much-reduced state which only provides a basic level of public service. The individual is now forced to take more responsibility for support which was previously provided through public services, while some are reduced to destitution.

There are elements of public sector reform, continuing since the global financial crisis of 2008, for example the focus on co-production and consumers, which highlight the need to develop new and different relationships with services users. However, the nature of public sector reforms has meant that the emphasis on consumers was essentially a superficial commitment to user interests which does not result in any significantly different relationships between public professionals and services users. This book has taken a critical perspective towards co-production, because it fits more into the goals of public sector reform and subsequent austerity policies with citizens encouraged to contribute their time, knowledge or assets to the provision of public services or even as an alternative to them.

The example of Arendt's *vita activa*, in relation to concepts of plurality, the public sphere and natality, is used to explain how to take democratic action giving an important theoretical dimension to this book. Although Arendt was writing in the 1950s, many of the questions which she tried to answer are very relevant to the early 21st century. This has been shown in why and how people try and take democratic political action. The case studies used in this book are intended to show why democratic professionals choose to take action.

Arendt's *vita activa* also helps to understand the contributions of democratic professionals to public services in a more explicit way. The concept of labouring as one of the basic activities of delivering public services helps to show that the element of caring runs through almost all public services. Similarly, seeing the contribution of work, as a skilled, knowledgeable activity which again is essential for high quality public services is important. These two elements are often invisible in descriptions of public services, especially in outsourced or privatised services, but they form a crucial part of what makes a high-quality public service. They do not fit into the commodified task-based approach to public services, which is increasingly prevalent.

The *vita activa* is relevant to the re-thinking of public services, which will be necessary in the future. The emphasis on action can be used to recognise that part of the process of delivering public services has to include some form of democracy. This has to be based on a belief in plurality and the importance of the public sphere. Both plurality and the public sphere are not uncontested terms and so will have to be re-defined in different settings, to inform preparation for action. Democratic professionals have to act on several different levels. Before looking at some of the factors that led democratic professionals to take action, the value in using an analysis of plurality, the public sphere and natality will be considered.

Plurality, the public sphere and natality

This book has argued that exploring plurality, the public sphere and natality provides a strategy for taking democratic action. At a time when the role of professionals and experts is being questioned, this may result in professional changes, even the rejection of the term professional. The impact of digitalisation on the delivery of public services is only just beginning to be felt. One perspective is that increased access to information will change the way in which professionals operate. Professionals will have to recognise that they will have to share their power, which is based on their expertise, with the users of services. This requires a transformation of their professional practice, made more complicated by digitalisation. A reflection on what plurality means in this changing context can start to highlight the need to value different sources of expertise.

Plurality should inform the creation of expertise as a joint enterprise between democratic professionals and citizens. This may have to draw on different types of experience and research, the latter designed so that citizens can participate in the research process and not just be research subjects. For example, it might be creating different evaluation methods to assess the value of existing public services so that identifying the need for new public services will also draw on a range of methods to assess the needs of many communities. The specific use of a shared language has emerged as an important part of democratic professionalism and will have to play a role in drawing on different forms of expertise.

If an awareness of plurality is integrated into professional practices, this leads to an exploration of what the public sphere is and what it might become. One of the strong arguments for using the *vita activa* is that Arendt's analysis of the public and private spheres is relevant to an understanding of many of the challenges facing public services in the 21st century. The demand for individualised services in health and social care is one of the challenges facing future public services. This conflicts with an earlier underlying principle of public services in the Welfare State, which based public services provision on a universal, collective responsibility, funded by state and tax-based funds.

This book has asserted that public services are part of the public sphere, so that action to strengthen and expand the public sphere will benefit public services. In a period when the nature of the state is changing and becoming less responsible for the maintenance of a public sphere, it will require action by democratic professionals in partnership with citizens to reclaim and redefine the public sphere. Drawing on plurality, the public sphere will have to become more inclusive with a wider recognition of how this inclusivity can be established and maintained. This is in contrast to the role of the Consolidation State or permanent austerity state which is establishing a much more exclusive public sphere through legislation and public policies, which seek to restrict and exclude citizens. This can be seen in the 'hostile environment' created by immigration policies which have resulted in many citizens being denied access to public services in the UK.

Yet, even if democratic professionals start to inform their search for action adopting plurality together with the need to renew the public sphere, this will not be enough to decide to take action. The belief in the need to take action has to be supported by an understanding of what action can achieve. In a period when the public sphere is being eroded and the power and corruption of the private sector is becoming more obvious, it is not always immediately clear what action to take. This is where the concept of natality is useful, because it draws on a wider belief that the creation of the new contributes to a hope for the future. It helps to believe in the value of an alternative future vision.

In addition, the belief in action has to be understood in relation to agency, which is closely linked to natality, the belief in newness. Highly relevant for informing future action in public services is the view of agency as defined by the temporal experience of an individual. Public services have evolved over time. Individual and collective memories of public services feature in the lives of users and democratic professionals. How democratic professionals use their personal and professional agency to take action is rooted in these memories. It will inform what happens in the future.

The reasons why democratic professionals take action

In order to understand what has made democratic professionals take action, this section will analyse the factors that contributed to the creation of democratic professional practice. There are several themes emerging from the case studies, which provide useful insights into why democratic professionals have taken action both now and in the past.

Understanding what lay behind the setting up of many of the case studies discussed in previous chapters provides some insight into the pre-conditions to rethinking public services and what causes public professionals to create new ways of working with service users. Also significant is whether the initiative was set up by one public professional or whether a group or team worked together to design and create a new public service. Understanding these processes will help to identify the support and training needed to further develop the practice of democratic professionalism.

Reaction to marketisation and privatisation

Several of the democratic professional case studies are reactions to increased marketisation and the threats of privatisation in a sector. The Social Workers Action Network and its Manifesto was drawn up by social workers in response to the problems facing social work and demanding that social work should aim to work towards social justice. As a profession with a long tradition of radical action, which has regularly challenged the position of social workers, the use of a network and a manifesto was a way of taking action in the current context of public sector reforms.

Similarly, the Gold Paper, written by a group of democratic professionals in Goldsmiths University, London was a reaction to the UK Government's Higher Education Green Paper 'Fulfilling our potential: teaching excellence, social mobility, and student choice' (2015) and other changes that had been taking place in higher education since the imposition of student loans. It was a way of challenging the proposed marketisation and privatisation of higher education by focusing on what a single university could provide in a more inclusive and progressive way.

The Cooperative University was also a response to reforms in higher education, which lecturers at the University of Lincoln felt threatened the future of public universities. An earlier research project, which had developed the concept of Student as Producer, recognised that students and lecturers are academic workers in the co-production of critical-practical knowledge. This became an organising principle for teaching and learning across the University of Lincoln. As a response to the increases in university tuition fees and reduced funding for Arts, Humanities and Social Sciences, the Social Science Centre was established in 2011. It uses a cooperative constitutional model and is a democratically run organisations owned by its members. At the same time as these changes were taking place, Cooperatives UK, an organisation representing and promoting cooperatives, was discussing the feasibility of setting up a cooperative university at its annual congress.

Responding to crisis

Another trigger for democratic professionals to develop a new initiative was in response to a crisis, whether in terms of a crisis for a public institution or a crisis where the formal public institutional response was either inadequate or non-existent. The occupation of Croxteth School in 1982/3 was a response, led by parents, to the threat of closure by Liverpool Education Committee. As a campaign had already been set up to counter plans to close the school, the action to occupy the school was another step in this campaign and teachers joined what turned into a three-year occupation to enable the school to continue functioning.

More recently, several projects have been set up which incorporate democratic elements into their design and seek to develop services for refugees and migrants, which public authorities have been unwilling to take responsibility for. The Liverpool Social Work Handbook for Refugees and Asylum Seekers was a direct response by social work students to working for Asylum Aid, an NGO, and realising that social workers needed more information if they were to be successful in supporting refugees and migrants. This was an initiative which worked with existing agencies and organisations, but Social Work without Borders was set up in response to the lack of coordinated action to look after the safeguarding of young refugees and migrants in the Calais Refugee camp. The organisation grew from an initiative taken by two women social workers who worked with volunteers in the camp.

Architects for Social Housing was set up in response to the public housing crisis in London by a woman architect who organised a collective of architects, planners, designers to develop technical support for communities on public housing estates threatened with re-development and the destruction of the existing housing stock. The way in which this group has mobilised professional expertise has taken a wider brief by working with communities to challenge the image of public housing as part of a campaign to use brownfield sites for new housing.

StreetDoctors was created as a result of trainee doctors identifying a need when teaching first aid to young people in Liverpool young offenders' service. This involved trainee doctors re-interpreting their training role in delivering first aid training to young people, to better meet the needs of young people at risk of violence. They identified the need for better provision of information and training about the effect of knife injuries. By thinking more widely about skills development for young people and recognising the knowledge that the young people possessed about their own communities, they trained young people in co-facilitating so that young people and trainee doctors could train groups together.

Primary schools located near to the Grenfell Tower responded to the needs of children and families after the fire by providing practical and psychological support. Technically, this was outside the remit of a primary school. However, schools took action through adopting a more holistic approach to their remit and this resulted in the creation of a caring and supporting environment which is helping families to survive a major disaster.

Understanding different life worlds

Other projects, several set up in the 1970s and 1980s, were attempts by democratic professionals to use creativity to help young people to understand and express their own life worlds. They made explicit links between schools and local communities. A London teacher, Chris Searle, worked with students at Stepney School in the 1980s using a critical pedagogy approach, which enabled students to make sense of the world in which they were living through creative writing. In a similar way, the Cockpit Arts project ran a series of out-of-school, after-school and holiday clubs between 1979 and 1985, which enabled young people to use photography as a way of expressing themselves.

Community health projects applied a similar approach to community health issues, where public health professionals worked with communities to identify ways of responding to their health needs and making public health services more accessible. Sometimes, these focused on a particular health issue or in many cases worked with communities on exploring what health actually meant to them and the factors that affected a particular community.

New initiatives or specific research projects

New initiatives created in response to a wider goal often provide opportunities for democratic professionals to take action and to develop new ways of delivering services, working closely with services users. These may be part of much wider goals, but they provide a space for re-thinking services and understanding some of the processes needed to work in different ways.

The 'Design for Carbon Reduction' is an example of an initiative which was the result of several wider campaigns and initiatives. Ezio Mantini, a specialist in design for everyday life, with colleagues from Parsons School of Design, a private New York art and design college, called for more collaboration between social networks and public services and innovation policies. This was taken up by the London-based University of the Arts and Camden Council. For the University of the Arts the call provided a rationale for a research-based practice project for students. For Camden Council, a research partnership with the UAL, provided a way of helping local people to reduce their carbon emissions.

The 'Gutter to Gulf' project was part of an academic project, where lecturers and students worked together, which was initiated by Jane Wolff, a lecturer at the Faculty of Architecture, Landscape and Design, Toronto University. After she had worked with a grassroots organisation in New Orleans, she recognised that there was a lack of information about the city's water and drainage systems, which would block any democratic attempts to re-build the city. She involved her students and colleagues in a research project, which documented and explained the city water and drainage systems and made the information available in a language which citizens, architects, planners and policy makers could all understand. This is another example of the importance of language in democratic professionalism.

The 'Risk Assessment' project, part of the Leeds-based democratic professionalism research project and funded by the Economic and Social Research Council, was set up as a way of exploring how risk assessment is practised and how service users could influence the process, drawing on their expertise through experience. This action was the result of initial discussions about what constituted democratic professionalism and how it could be implemented in mental health services.

The City of Leeds aims to become a child-friendly city. This has influenced the way in which the social services department in Leeds City Council approached a review of its children's services. It identified the problems of 'looked-after children' and, rather than design another service, decided to find ways of engaging the expertise of families in caring for children who might otherwise have gone into 'care'.

Research

Research into the needs of communities experiencing discrimination and identifying ways of meeting these needs has provided the basis of new democratic professionalism practice. The National Union of Students researched the presence of Black and Minority Ethnic groups in academia in the United Kingdom, and the results informed the setting up of the 'Dismantling the Master's House' campaign. This has triggered debate and extended awareness within universities globally. It also came at a time when the #RhodesMustFall campaign, which also questioned the dominance of a white view of history, was growing.

The Silent University was set up by a group of refugees working with the Tate Gallery and the Delfina Foundation. It was a reaction to the enforced silence of refugees and migrants, who are unable to use their professional knowledge, skills and expertise, because their qualifications are not recognised in the countries they have moved to. This has expanded by encouraging new branches of the Silent University to be set up in other countries.

Reflection around professional practice

The role of reflection by democratic professionals on their professional practice is one of the most powerful factors which has led to new forms of action. This may be triggered by dissatisfaction with existing professional practice or a sense that wider issues are not being addressed.

The Early Years profession, a relatively new profession, has spent time in developing and reflecting on how it can develop a new form of professional practice, which is based on working in a democratic way. The Reggio Emilia Network of Early Years has a core belief in the value of listening to children, which has influenced its professional practice. It adopted a pedagogy of listening which respects the personal expression of each child.

Nursing is a much older profession. In the 1970s groups of nurses started to reflect on their professional practice, because they felt that the healthcare system was not meeting the needs of patients. This led to a greater awareness of the nature of professional relationships between nurses and doctors. The creation of the Radical Nurses Group was an action taken to provide support for nurses who wanted to rethink their professional practice. Many of their findings have informed the development of the nursing profession since then.

In a similar way, social workers affected by the impact of the corporatisation of public services have started to rethink the way in which social workers can provide advice in different settings and in different types of organisations. Part of this process has involved social workers thinking critically about their existing professional practice and whether it meets the needs of service users.

An even more radical rethink of professional practice led to the creation of forensic architecture, a sub-division of architecture. A British–Israeli architect, through his research, realised how architecture and planning were used to deny human rights as part of Israeli actions towards the Palestinians. This awareness led to the application of architectural skills and techniques as a form of forensic practice for communities trying to establish the truth in human rights violations.

The National Union of Teachers used its reflections on professional and political practice to develop a manifesto to campaign for progressive changes in education. Perhaps as important was the emphasis on the need to renew the union through increased organising. Trade unions and professional organisations play an important role in stimulating reflection on professional practice.

In summary, there are several factors that contribute to the development of professional democratic practice. Many will complement each other but the impact of a crisis or how to meet needs which are not currently being met by public services are ones that most often lead to new democratic professional practice.

Democratic professionalism and women

The use of Arendt's *vita activa* provides a way of seeing public services that values the processes of labour and work, most often provided by women. The majority of public professionals are women. This book has tried to highlight the position of women in institutions and how this might affect their taking action. Some of the projects analysed were set up by women and then often taken over by groups or collectives, which incorporate a more democratic way of working among democratic professionals as well as with service users. More needs to be understood about how women and men decide to take action in these contexts. The belief in natality and the value of change is a good starting point, but how professional agency is interpreted can be influenced by many factors. Black and Minority Ethnic women also make up the majority of the workforce in some public services, and the actions that they have taken already need to be made more visible.

The search for a more plural approach to expertise is one way of valuing caring expertise in a more positive way. There are examples of how the experiences of women have been incorporated into the design and delivery of public services, for example, some forms of cancer treatment, but the longer-term effects of valuing family and caring expertise may change the perception of caring more fundamentally.

Status of democracy in public services

This book has explored the term 'democratic professional' in relation to its history and current practice. It is a relatively new term, and this section aims to answer the question 'What does democracy in public services look like?' by drawing together elements of democratic professional practice. These sometimes emerge through a project, but they often require extensive support from the service users, citizens and democratic professionals. New changes in professional practice that are the result of operating and relating in different ways take time to consolidate. There needs to be a constant process of evolution.

The valuing of expertise emerges as a strong element of democratic practice. The main democratic elements in the Leeds City Council 'Family Valued' programme are about valuing the caring expertise in families. In order to facilitate this expertise, the way in which space is organised, how meetings are conducted and how families are given time and space to develop solutions to their own problems can all be seen as being part of democratic practice. This is in contrast to a more conventional approach, where professionals provide the solutions.

The Cooperative University has developed a concept of 'Student as Producer' which helped to re-define the relationships between students and lecturers and how this has contributed to the creation of knowledge. Even so, the practice that the research informed has taken time to establish. It shows how the expectations of both students and lecturers take time to consolidate into a more democratic practice.

The main democratic element of the Gold Report was that it created a vision of Goldsmiths University as a holistic system, where everyone, from support staff to director, is recognised as playing an important part in running the institution. This creates a sense of value throughout the university. It depends on all staff and students being treated with respect and provided with opportunities to influence decision-making. Similarly, the Silent University provides refugees and migrants with opportunities to use their expertise and to be valued for it.

Listening and valuing is emerging as part of democratic practice. The Reggio Emelia Network of Early Years is explicit about the importance of listening. There are different ways in which this can be put into practice. Chris Searle and the publication of 'Stepney Worlds' used a critical pedagogy which enabled young people to express themselves and be listened to. The Cockpit Arts used photography with a similar result.

Access to information and expertise has provided an important focus for many of the case studies. The development of the Liverpool social work handbook for refugees and asylum seekers was a response by social workers to their own lack of information and inability to meet the needs of refugees. The 'Gutter to Gulf' project made information available to many groups within New Orleans in an accessible way so that everyone could participate in democratic dialogue about the future of the city.

The creation of 'Social Workers Without Borders' was a way of making social work and legal expertise available to children who were unable to access it in refugee camps in Europe. Similarly, Architects for Social Housing have made their technical expertise available to people living in public housing schemes, but the group has worked in a way that enables the residents to campaign and take part in consultations with a stronger knowledge base.

Language emerges from almost all these case studies as being central to effective democratic practice. The 'Gutter to Gulf' practice was specifically focused on finding a language which all groups – grass roots organisations, architects, planners, politicians – could use to discuss the future development of New Orleans by sharing an understanding of the water systems. The democratic professionalism in the mental health services project identified the importance of language in redefining relationships between professionals and service users.

The National Union of Teachers was more explicit in addressing a democratic element of professional practice by taking a more active part in a general election campaign. It developed a manifesto for its members to raise the awareness of parents and other stakeholders about what a future education policy should look like.

There are several elements of a democratic professionalism. Initially it may be about providing access to expertise in different settings and services. One of the most important is the use of knowledge and skills in a way that involves citizens and service users in the creation and application of expertise. This is based on identifying and valuing diverse sources of expertise.

The importance of listening and valuing informs the practice of democratic professionalism. This is dependent on an analysis of different publics and identifying ways of working with them to meet their needs. This creates a wider vision of who should be included in the public sphere.

The process of listening and valuing depends on the use of language and its importance in creating a democratic space which can be defended against further incursions of the new market and Consolidation state and what is left of the Welfare State.

Working with other organisations

Another dimension of democratic professionalism is the extent to which other agencies and organisations are involved. If a more holistic approach to the delivery of public services is adopted, which democratic professionalism encompasses, collaboration with other organisations will have to inform some of the actions taken.

Leeds City Council social services department worked with the Family Rights Group (FRG), an NGO, and other new organisations and networks which have been set up to provide training and support to social workers involved in working with a 'restorative' approach. FRG introduced new ways of working and provided training and new forms of expertise for social workers.

The University of the Arts found that it had to work collaboratively to deliver their project to develop new services so that local residents would adopt ways of living which reduced carbon emissions. Similarly, Camden Council found that it had to collaborate with an academic institution if it was to answer some of its questions about how to encourage its citizens to adopt a more carbon-free way of living. The Cooperative University works closely with Cooperative UK, the umbrella organisation in the UK which supports cooperative ways of working.

Social Workers without Borders was created as the result of the merger of several organisations working with refugees in Europe. StreetDoctors also created its own organisation which now runs the training sessions and does developmental work.

Much democratic professionalism is dependent on collaborative and partnership working. It can also lead to the creation of new organisations, often non-governmental organisations. This will have to be discussed, because it raises questions about how public services will be delivered in the future. Remembering the importance of the public sphere may be a guiding principle in creating future organisations. New organisations must be a part of the public sphere if they are to deliver public services in an inclusive way.

Training and development needed

What has emerged from these case studies and examples about how action was taken and how to maintain a democratic practice, has implications for the training and development of democratic professionals and service users. Transforming practice depends on new skills and the rethinking of existing practice. Several case studies had training integrated into the projects and the success of the projects was dependent on democratic professionals developing new expertise.

Other projects have used training programmes to support democratic professionals in working in a more inclusive way. The 'Family Valued' programme has trained social workers in a restorative practice approach. The Family Rights Group runs training in how to facilitate Family Group Conferences. Both these approaches require training of public professionals if they are to be successful because they question existing social work practice and aim to change some of the assumptions and ways of operating of social work professionals.

The project 'Design for Carbon Reduction' shows how training had to be incorporated into the project so that students and communities were prepared to work in different ways. Students from the University of the Arts (UAL) had recognised that they needed to be prepared for working with community groups. The students had only worked in product design but not service design. UAL had to re-orientate them and drew on students from an MA in Applied Imagination to provide peer support. Both technical product skills and skills to work with communities were needed.

The Cooperative University and the Silent University use workshops as a way of operating in which everyone contributes to teaching and learning. The 'Dismantling the Master's House' campaign was supported by lectures and workshops. Part of the NUT's promotion of democratic professionalism was to provide training in union organising at local level as well as skills to negotiate at local level in reaction to the imposition of school-be-school bargaining on the teaching profession.

In future, training and professional development will have to start to address how to change professional practice through collaborative working with different stakeholders. At the core will be the creation of a more holistic view of services being delivered and the involvement of professionals at all levels – service delivery, organisation, democratic management and participation. This will require professionals to have a wider range of skills and more confidence to use the expertise in different settings. It will also need greater user involvement in public services.

Types of support needed

This book has shown, through a series of examples and case studies that the concept of democratic professionalism can be used to create a new form of professionalism in which relations between users and professionals operate in a more democratic

Table 4: Case-studies by service

Public service	Case study/example
Education/schools	Reggio Emilia
	Women teachers in Brazil
	Stepney School
	NUT organising
	Cockpit Arts
	Schools response to Grenfell fire
	Croxteth School
Higher education	Cooperative University
	Gold Report
	The Silent University
	Dismantling His Master's House
Social work	Leeds City Council/Family Rights Group
	Liverpool Social Work Handbook for migrants/refugees
	Risk assessment in mental health services
	Social Work without Borders
Architecture/design	Carbon reduction
	'Gutter to Gulf'
	Architects for Social Housing
	Assemble and Granby Street
	Forensic Architecture
Healthcare	Women's health centres
	StreetDoctors
	Sickle Cell Centres
	Radical Nurses Group

way. There are some differences in the responses of different public professionals to democratic professionalism.

The majority of case studies were in either schools or higher education. This may be because there are elements of democratic professionalism which are most clearly identified in educational practice. Public pedagogy plays an important role in many projects, but it is most easily articulated in education. This has implications for training in other public services.

The healthcare sector may be one of the most difficult in which to create democratic professional initiatives because of the power of healthcare systems and other healthcare professionals. The democratic professional health initiatives that have been recounted all had a community focus where the relationships between public professionals are mediated by their relationships with communities.

Social workers also work in bureaucratic structures but the role of the state as a provider of social welfare services is changing, and this has forced social workers to rethink their professional roles. In addition, the impact of refugees and migrants in many European societies has made the providers of social services think more creatively about the types of services needed.

Architects are actively involved in rethinking their professional roles, partly because the public role of architects is under scrutiny. The commercialisation of land and building developments has made many architects part of a highly commercialised process. In the UK, local authorities no longer have public architecture departments. This has made architects who believe in playing a public role develop alternative ways of operating within a democratic process. The creativity with which some architects now address the development of an inclusive public sphere shows how democratic professionalism can flourish outside a formal public sector.

As this brief survey of the case studies used shows, some public services are more likely to be able to develop new democratic practices than others although many public sector professionals may be interested in reflecting on their practice. Budget cuts may trigger different ways of working although a growing private sector presence may make this process more difficult. Private companies are driven by a for-profit motive rather than a public, democratic ethos. Other services, such as health care may be affected by the relationship between key professionals. For example, nurse–patient relationships are still influenced by the relationship between nurses and doctors.

Support for democratic professionalism

Democratic professionals who want to pursue a democratic way of operating and consolidating their existing practice will have to find ways of establishing support with like-minded public professionals and other groups working to improve public services and making the public sphere more inclusive.

The importance of developing democratic ways of working in teams is a way of strengthening more democratic ways of working with clients. Recognising the value of the whole team, whether front-line or back office, creates a more holistic view of how a public service can be delivered and contributes to a more pluralistic view of different stakeholders.

Some sectors already have some forms of support available for democratic professionals. The Expansive Education Network was set up to give validity to student views. It works to establish lifelong learning by acknowledging that education is about more than passing exams. This network provides a foundation for teachers to work in a more democratic way with students. It redefines teachers as learners who are looking for and researching better pedagogic outcomes.

Communities of practice are an established way of developing professional practice and they will continue to provide support to public professionals who want to develop different ways of working with service users. Different stakeholders can form a community of practice. Within a school this could be parents, teachers and local people who choose to work towards improving some aspect of service provision. Examples of this include the increased integration of refugees and migrants into educational systems/schools or advice centres. The stakeholders have to agree on what they would like to improve, share their own perceptions of existing practices and work together to break down barriers. For public professionals this has to involve listening and sharing ideas and solutions as well as responding to criticisms of existing professional practice.

The concept of ecologies of practice has been developed as a way of understanding professional development and identity. Ecologies of practice show that different practices are related to a whole and so are interdependent. Perhaps more importantly, it shows that different practices are organic and change in the same way that living things change. Based on principles of ecology, professional practices are related to each other through networks, interdependent relations between practices, their diversity, development through stages and a dynamic balance which creates a process of self-regulation (Kemmis et al, 2009). Although initially developed for use in education, ecologies of practice are being used in other sectors to understand and develop professional practice. This is the reason why the approach may be valuable in supporting democratic professionalism because it links many different practices together, recognises that these practices change over time and are dynamic. It should be considered not just as a way of supporting democratic professionals in one public service but also across services and sectors.

Trade unions and professional associations have a vital role to play in the promotion of democratic professional practice. Although some trade unions and professional organisations have already started to reflect on how democratic professionalism can be supported (Lethbridge, 2015), this work will compete with more immediate concerns about jobs and employment security. It will require a much greater awareness among trade unions and professional associations about how they can help to shape future professional practice.

The creation of effective alliances will be at the centre of transformation. Training and professional development will have to start to address how to change professional practice through collaborative working with different stakeholders. This has already started but not necessarily with a democratic focus. At the core will be the creation of a more holistic view of services being delivered and the involvement of professionals at all levels – service delivery, organisation, democratic management and participation.

Universities are also presented with the challenge of how to engage with these issues when training professionals. There are opportunities in identifying democratic professional practices and to engage new professionals with the concept of democratic professionalism in the development of their professional identity. However, university training courses are already under attack by the move towards on-the-job training.

There are many examples of democratic professionalism found in various countries, across public services and at different time periods. These can be a source of inspiration for democratic professionals interested in taking action. For example, Brazil introduced new democratic structures in public services after 1988. Citizens were given a role in the public management of public services and these examples are helpful in identifying new types of structures and the support needed.

Implications for future public services

Democratic professionalism is an important concept which has been refined over the last thirty years and should be seen as part of a longer tradition of questioning professional power. The current interest in democratic professionalism is significant because public sector reforms were influenced by the dissatisfaction felt by some public service users in the services they received. For example, parents of children taken into care by social workers did not feel that their rights were recognised. The rationale for public sector reforms was the need for users or consumers of public services to assert their rights to a choice of services. This situation often set service users against the professionals providing the services, exacerbating problems of professional power and undermining public sector professionals.

Several examples of taking action have resulted in the creation of new organisations rather than a change of practice in an existing public service. This has implications for the struggle to maintain and develop public services. If new organisations are created which are practicing a form of democratic professionalism because it has not been possible to create a similar practice in a public institution, this may undermine existing public services. There are risks in this approach but the importance of trying and testing out approaches to democratic professionalism can justify the creation of a separate organisation. However, in the long term, the aim should be to incorporate the new practice or new organisation into public services.

There are also risks of mainstreaming new practices which create democratic relationships between service users and democratic professionals without more extensive changes in relationships and structures in public services. There are examples of democratic professionalism, for example, community health projects in the 1980s and 1990s, which were incorporated into existing public services. They have often struggled to survive.

There is a history of how public services and the public sector have reacted to community-based ways of working, often through a process of co-optation of community members or by diluting the value given to community views. The experiences of local government community workers who worked with communities to campaign for improved services but came into conflict with other local authority workers who did not share their community-based approach need to be remembered. The emphasis on consulting and working with local communities was taken on by many New Labour initiatives but the commitment by parts of the public sector to working through and establishing new, more democratic relationships with local communities was limited (Mayo, Hoggett and Miller, 2007). Working towards democratic professionalism needs to be accompanied by campaigning for more democratic structures in the public sector and public ownership. This requires a political commitment and will.

Many changes are starting to take place in public services, but in a context which does not necessarily support a democratic form of working. This can be seen in the limited debate that has taken place about the influence of service users in new systems of regulation. The only way this question can be resolved is through wider involvement of service users in public services with public professionals. Although public sector reform supposedly addresses this through the introduction of consumerism and choice, this is an individualised approach which does not facilitate a wider democratic contribution of service users to the delivery of public services.

There is also the issue of language, which has seen to be central to effective democratic professionalism. There are terms which are part of a public sector reform and austerity agenda, for example, 'co-production', which can be confused with elements of democratic professionalism. The use of family expertise to support a child so that 'care' by the local authority is avoided has been shown to be part of democratic professionalism, because it values family expertise but this can also be interpreted as families providing resources for public services.

Limits to democratic professionalism

Although democratic professionalism can be seen as part of a longer historical process of challenging professional power, its future will be strongly influenced by the current state of public services and the continued attacks on the integrity and judgements of public professionals. Part of the rationale of public management reforms was the failure of public services to meet the needs of service users. However, the conversion of services users into consumers combined with the introduction of business models framed by austerity policies has resulted in the reduction in the size, scope and quality of public services and their reduced ability to meet the needs of service users. The examples and case studies discussed in this book show that new and varied ways of meeting the needs of service users as well as changing ways of using professional expertise can be introduced in the context of public management reforms.

Chapter 1 included a discussion of what democratic professionalism is not and points to the risks involved in introducing more equitable ways of sharing professional power and meeting the needs of service users when these values are not actively recognised in the practice of institutions. The public professional may be left exposed in terms of not being able to provide an adequate service and will not be able to ensure that any future contacts between public service institutions and service users will be democratically informed. At the moment, there is uncertainty about the future role of the state and the delivery of public services. For the UK, the future of public services will depend on decisions about its future relations with the European Union. For other countries, the influence of regressive monetary policies and the role of the private sector in public service provision remain strong influences on future public services. There is a growing interest in alternatives to conventional neo-liberal economics accompanied by a growing realisation that growing inequalities of wealth and harsh austerity policies are undermining the social and economic fabric of society. At the same time right-wing political parties are winning an increased share of votes in regional and national elections.

In the UK there seem to be two possible public service scenarios. The optimistic one is where there is some nationalisation of utilities and other service sectors, greater investment in existing public services including public service workers, accompanied by demands for a greater democratic involvement of citizens in public services. With these changes would come demands for a greater practice of democratic professionalism and more understanding of how both public professionals and service users can engage with each other in a more democratic way. This would have to be supported by other institutional changes which provide new opportunities for the expression of democracy. If local government was subject to a process of renewal, then its existing democratic structures could provide a place to begin new ways of introducing democratic professionalism into public service delivery.

The alternative scenario, which in the UK would almost certainly accompany a 'hard' Brexit exit from the EU, would result in the intensification of austerity policies, continued reductions in funding for public services and a greater emphasis on individual responsibility rather than collective and universal benefits. Continued cuts in funding and limited investment in the future of public services, especially the workforce, will make attempts to expand the practice of democratic professionalism more difficult. It requires, as shown earlier in this chapter, time to listen and work with service users, training for public professionals and the development of partnerships with stakeholders. In this context, attempts to practice democratic professionalism will be more individually focused, making public professionals more vulnerable to criticism and often lacking support. However, it is worth revisiting the vision of Hannah Arendt's *vita activa* with its three elements – labour, work and action – that can be applied to public services. The need for democratic action as part of the process of delivering public services will remain, both now and in the future, and has to be seen as part of a wider political framework.

This raises some of the questions about the elements of agency in democratic professionalism that were discussed in Chapter 5. Democratic professionalism is the result of both individual agency and institutional agency. It cannot be seen as something that is just 'required' of a public professional. Some of the problems caused by co-creation and co-production are the result of co-production being imposed as a top-down policy rather than emerging as a bottom-up reaction to inadequate involvement of services users in public services. In this sense, the use of democratic professionalism as an instant 'solution' to some of the problems of public service delivery will not work. Again, much can be learnt from the experience of introducing progressive ways of working in, for example, schools, which are often diluted without a commitment to a more fundamental rethinking of education.

Democratic professionalism within a wider political framework

As this book has shown, Hannah Arendt's *vita activa*, which uses the search for plurality, an expansion of the public sphere and a belief in the value of working towards new visions to inform future democratic action for public services, contributes to a more detailed view of how and why people take action. Although applied to public services, the strategy can also be applied to wider struggles for democratic expression.

The future of public services needs to be shaped by public professionals and service users working together, sharing knowledge, respecting each other and taking joint responsibility for addressing problems. The development of democratic professionalism is at an early stage. It will require a much greater awareness among trade unions and professional associations about how they can help to shape future professional practice. The creation of effective alliances will be at the centre of the transformation, by involving wider campaigns and social movements. It will also contribute to wider political campaigns and the formation of stronger political alliances to challenge the shift towards right-wing populism and the failures of current economic policies. The promotion of democratic professionalism should be seen in this broader context of economic, social and political change.

References

Ainley, P. (2001) From a National System Locally Administered to a National System Nationally Administered: The New Leviathan in Education and Training in England, *The Journal of Social Policy*, 3(3): 457–476.

Ainley, P. (2016) *Betraying a generation: How education is failing young people*, Bristol: Policy Press.

Alford, J. and Yates, S. (2015) Co-production of public services in Australia: the roles of government organisations and co-producers, *Australian Journal of Public Administration*, 75(2): 159–175.

Allen, P. (2013) The professionalisation of politics makes our democracy less representative and less accessible, *Democratic audit,* 11 September 2013.

Architects for Social Housing (2018) ASH Architects 4 Social Housing http://architectsforsocialhousing.co.uk/ (Accessed 30 November 2018).

Arendt, H. (1958) *The Human Condition*, Chicago: University of Chicago Press.

Arnstein, S. (1969) A ladder of citizen participation, *Journal of the American Planning Association*, 35(4): 216–224.

Arts, W. and Gelissen, J. (2002) Three worlds of welfare capitalism or more? A state of the art report, *Journal of European Social Policy*, 12(2): 137–158.

Assemble (2018) *Granby Four Streets 2013–17*, Assemble https://assemblestudio.co.uk/ (Accessed 30 November 2018).

Avis, J. (2003) Re-thinking trust in a performative culture: the case of education, *Journal of Education Policy*, 18(3): 315–332.

Baginsky, M., Moriarty, J., Manthorpe, J., Stevens, M., MacInnes, T. and Nagendran, T. (2009) *Social workers' workload survey messages from the frontline findings from the 2009 survey and interviews with senior managers*, London: Social Work Task Force.

Ball, S.J. (2008) Performativity, privatisation, professionals and the state, in Cunningham B. (ed.) *Exploring professionalism*, Bedford Way Papers London: Institute of Education.

Bartels, K.P.R. (2012) Public Encounters: the history and future of face-to-face contact between public professionals and citizens, *Public Administration*, 91(2): 469–483.

Beebeejaun, Y., Durose, C., James Rees, J. and Richardson, J. (2015) Public harm or public value? Towards coproduction in research with communities, *Environment and Planning C: Government and Policy*, 33(3): 552–565.

Bertilsson, M. (1990) The welfare state, the professions and citizens, in R. Torstandahl and M. Burrage (eds) *The formation of professions knowledge, state and strategy*, London: Sage.

Biesta, G. (2007) Why 'what works' won't work: evidence-based practice and the democratic deficit of educational research, *Educational Theory*, 57(1): 1–22.

Biesta, G. (2010) Why 'what works' still won't work: from evidence-based education to value-based education, *Studies in Philosophy and Education*, 29(5): 491–503.

Biesta, G. (2012) Becoming public: public pedagogy, citizenship and the public sphere, *Social and Cultural Geography*, 13(7): 683–697.

Biesta, G. (2015) The role of beliefs in teacher agency, *Teachers and Teaching: Theory and Practice*, 21(6): 624–640.

Bogdanor, V. (2011) *Britain in the 20th century: The attempt to construct a socialist common wealth, 1945–1951*, Lecture at Gresham College, London, November 2011.

Boyte, H. (2010) Constructive politics as public work: organising the literature, *Political Theory*, 39(5): 630–660.

Boyte, H. (ed.) (2015) *Democracy's education public work, citizenship and the future of colleges and universities*, Nashville: Vanderbilt University Press.

Brown, P. (2007) Trusting in the new NHS: instrumental versus communicative action, *Sociology of Health and Illness*, 30(3): 349–363.

Buchan, J. and Ball, J. (2011) Evaluating the impact of a new pay system on nurses in the UK, *Journal of Clinical Nursing*, 20(1–2): 50–9.

Burawoy, M. (2005) For public sociology, *Sociology*, 70(1): 4–28.

Butler, J. (1988) Performative acts and gender constitution: an essay in phenomenology and feminist theory, *Theatre Studies*, 40(4): 519–531.

Calas, M.B. and Smircich, L. (1996) From the 'woman's point of view': towards a feminist organization studies, in S. Clegg, C. Hardy and W. Nord (eds) *Handbook of organization studies*, London: Sage, 218–256.

Calas, M.B. and Smircich, L. (2006) From the 'woman's point of view' ten years later: towards a feminist organization studies, in S. Clegg, C. Hardy, W. Nord and T. Lawrence (eds) *Handbook of organization studies* (2nd edition) London: Sage: 284–346.

Cambrosio, A., Limoges, C. and Hoffman E. (1992) Expertise as a network: a case study of the controversies over the environmental release of genetically engineered organisms, in N. Stehr and R.V. Ericson (eds) *The culture and power of knowledge*, Berlin: Walter de Gruyter: 341–361.

Carspecken, III F. (1987) *The campaign to save Croxteth Comprehensive: An ethnographic study of a protest movement*, Submitted for the Degree of Doctor of Philosophy University of Aston in Birmingham.

Civil Service Code, (2010) *Civil service code*, London: HM Government https://www.gov.uk/government/publications/civil-service-code (Accessed 30 November 2018).

Collins, H. (2014) *Are we all scientific experts now?* Cambridge: Polity Press.

Collins, P.H. and Bilge S. (2016) *Intersectionality*, Cambridge: Polity Press.

Collins, R. (1990) Changing conceptions in the sociology of the professions, in R. Torstandahl and M. Burrage (eds) *The formation of professions knowledge, state and strategy*, London: Sage: 11–13.

Cooley, M. (1987) *Architect or bee? The human/technology relationship*, Slough: Langley Technical Services.

Cortes Camarillo, G. (2002) Review: Chris Searle (1998) None but Our Words: Critical Literacy in Classroom and Community, *Forum Qualitative Sozialforschung/Forum: Qualitative Social Research*, 3(4): 31–39.

Crossley, N. (1998) R D Laing and the British anti–psychiatry movement: a socio-historical analysis, *Social Science and Medicine*, 47(7): 877–889.

Crouch, C. (2015) *The knowledge corrupters*, Cambridge: Polity Press.

Dale, J. and Foster, P. (2012) *Feminists and state welfare* (RLE Feminist Theory), London: Routledge.

Damaska, M.R. (1986) *The faces of justice and state authority: A comparative approach to the legal process*, New Haven: Yale University Press.

Davies, C. (1996) The sociology of the professions and the profession of gender, *Sociology*, 30(4): 661–678.

De Leeuw, E., Townsend, B., Martin, E., Jones, C.M. and Clavier C. (2013) Emerging theoretical frameworks for global health governance, in C. Clavier and E. de Leeuw (eds) *Health Promotion and the Policy Process*, Oxford: Oxford University Press: 104–130.

Democratic Professionalism and Mental Health Workshop (2016) Democratic professionalism and mental health workshop, *Seminar Series Reimagining Professionalism in mental health: towards co-production*, https://medhealth.leeds.ac.uk/info/1164/esrc_seminar_series/1971/seminar_1_university_of_leeds_5_january_2016 (Accessed 30 November 2018).

Department of Education and Science (1965) DES *Circular 7/65*, London: Department of Education and Science.

Dewdney, A. and Lister, M. (1988) *Youth, culture and photography*, Basingstoke: Macmillan Education.

Dewey, J. (1888) *The ethics of democracy*, Ann Arbor: Andrews and Company.

Dewey, J. (1916) *Democracy and education*, MacMillan Company.

Dewey, J. (1939/1989) *Freedom and culture democratic politics: communitarian, enlightened and participatory*, Prometheus Books.

Dewey, J. (1987) *The Later Works, 1925–1953: 1935–1937*, SIU Press.

Dietz, M. (1991) Hannah Arendt and feminist politics, in M.L. Shanley and C. Pateman (eds) *Feminist interpretations and political theory*, Cambridge: Polity Press.

DiMaggio, P.J. (1991) Constructing an organizational field as a professional project: U.S. art museums, 1920–1940, in W.W. Powell and P.J. DiMaggio (eds) *The new institutionalism in organizational analysis*, Chicago: University of Chicago Press: 267–292.

Dismantling the Master's House (2018) *Dismantling the Master's House*, http://www.dtmh.ucl.ac.uk/ (30 November 2018).

Durkheim, E. (1958) *Professional ethics and civic morals*, Westport Connecticut: Greenwood Press.

Dzur, D.W. (2004) Civic participation in professional domains: an introduction to the Symposium, *The Good Society Committee on the Political Economy of the Good Society*, 13(1): 3–4.

Dzur, A. (2008) *Democratic professionalism: Citizen participation and the reconstruction of professional ethics, identity and practice*, Pennsylvania: Pennsylvania State University Press.

Elmer, S. and Dening, G. (2015) Architects for social housing: fighting a political 'crisis', *Open Democracy*, vol 31, July.

Emirbayer, M. and Mische, A. (1998) What is agency? *American Journal of Sociology*, 104(4): 962–1023.

Engelen, E., Erturk, I., Froud, J. and Johal, S. (2012) *After the great complacence: Financial crisis and the politics of reform*, Oxford: Oxford University Press.

Ercan, S.A. and Dryzek, J.S. (2015) The reach of deliberative democracy: Special Issue: The Sites of Deliberative Democracy, *Policy Studies*, 36(3): 241–248.

Escobar, O. (2013) *Transformative practices: The political work of public engagement practitioners*, PhD in Politics University of Edinburgh.

Esping-Andersen, G. (1990) *The three worlds of welfare capitalism*, Cambridge: Polity Press.

Eteläpelto, A., Vähäsantanen, K., Hökkä, P. and Paloniemi, S. (2013) What is agency? Conceptualizing professional agency at work, *Educational Research Review*, 10(2013): 45–65

Expansive Education Network, (2015) What is expansive education? http://www.expansiveeducation.net/ (accessed 30 November 2018).

Eyal, G. (2013) For a sociology of expertise: the social origins of the autism epidemic, *American Journal of Sociology*, 118(4): 863–907.

Family Rights Group (2018) *Family Rights Group*, www.frg. org.uk

Family Rights Group, (2018) The Family Group Conference process, http://www.frg.org.uk/the-family-group-conference-process (accessed 30 November 2018).

Fassin, Y., Deprez, J., Van den Abeele, A. and Heene, A. (2017) Complementarities between stakeholder management and participative management: evidence from the Youth Care Sector, *Nonprofit and Voluntary Sector Quarterly*, 46(3): 586–606.

Ferguson, I. (2009) Another social work is possible: reclaiming the radical tradition, in I. Ferguson and R. Woodward (eds) (2009) *Radical social work in practice Making a difference*, Bristol: Policy Press.

Fieldgrass, J. (1992) *Partnerships in health promotion collaboration between the statutory and voluntary sectors*, London: Health Education Authority.

Fisher, P. and Lees, J. (2015) Narrative approaches in mental health: preserving the emancipatory tradition, *Health, An Interdisciplinary Journal for the Social Study of Health, Illness and Medicine*, 20(6): 599–615.

Flynn, N. (2007) *Public Administration* (5th edition), London: Sage.

Forensic Architecture (2018) Personal attendance at the Forensic Architecture *Counter Investigations exhibition* Institute of Contemporary Arts (ICA) https://www.ica.art/exhibitions/forensic-architecture-counter-investigations (Accessed 30 November 2018).

Forensic Architecture (2018a) About https://www.forensic-architecture.org/ (Accessed 30 November 2018).

Freire P. (1970) *The pedagogy of the oppressed*, London: Penguin.

Gaffney, D., Pollock, A., Dunnigan, M., Price, D. and Shaoul, J. (1999) PFI in the NHS: is there an economic case? *British Medical Journal*, vol 319, July: 48–51.

Garrett, P.M. (2009) *Transforming children's services? Social work, neoliberalism and the 'modern' world*, Maidenhead: Open University Press.

General Social Care Council (2010) *Code of practice*, London: General Social Care Council.

Giddens, A. (1979) *Central problems in social theory*, Cambridge: Polity Press.

Giddens, A. (1984) *The constitution of society: Outline of the theory of structuration*, Cambridge: Polity Press.

Gilbert, T.P. (2005) Impersonal trust and professional authority: exploring the dynamics, *Journal of Advanced Nursing*, 49(6): 568–577.

Gill, N., Singleton, V. and Waterton, C. (2017) The politics of policy practices, *The Sociological Review Monographs*, 65(2): 3–19.

(The) Gold Paper (2016) *The Gold Paper*, https://goldsmithsucu. wordpress.com/2016/04/11/the-gold-paper/ (Accessed 30 November 2018).

Goss, S. (2001) *Making local governance work: Networks, relationships and the management of change*, Basingstoke: Palgrave Macmillan.

Gramsci, A. (1971) *Selections from the prison notebooks*, London: Lawrence and Wishart.

(The) Guardian (2016) Children in the Calais refugee camp are at risk. Social workers must act, *The Guardian*, 22 June 2016.

Hardcastle, N-A.R., Usher, K.J. and Holmes, C.A. (2005) An overview of structuration theory and its usefulness for nursing research, *Nursing Philosophy*, 6(4): 223–234.

Hasted, C. (2012) How family group conferences have the power to change lives, *The Guardian*, 10 October 2012.

Hellowell, M. and Pollock, A.M. (2007) *Private finance, public deficits A report on the cost of PFI and its impact on health services in England*, Edinburgh: Centre for International Public Health Policy.

Henriksson, L., Wrede, S. and Burau, V. (2006) Understanding professional projects in welfare service work: revival of old professionalism? *Gender, Work and Organization*, 13(2): 174–192.

Hermann, C. and Flecker, J. (2012) *Privatization of public services*, London: Routledge.

Hoggett, P. Mayo, M. and Miller, C. (2006) Private passions, the public good and public service reform, *Social Policy and Administration*, 40(7): 758–773.

Hood, C., Scott, C. James, O. Jones, G. and Travers, T. (1999) *Regulation inside government: Waste watchers*, London; Oxford University Press.

Jasanoff, S. (2005) Judgement under siege: the three-body problem of expert legitimacy, in P. Weingart and S. Maasen (eds) *Democratization of expertise? Exploring novel forms of scientific advice in political decision-making: Sociology of the Sciences Yearbook*, Dordrecht: Kluwer: 209–224.

Jasanoff, S. (2016) *The ethics of invention: Technology and the human future*, New York: W.W. Norton and Company.

Jennings, L.B. and Da Matta, G.B. (2009) Rooted in resistance: women teachers constructing counter pedagogies in post-authoritarian Brazil, *Teaching Education*, 20(3): 215–228.

Joas, H. (1996) *The creativity of action*, Cambridge: Polity Press.

Jones, C., Ferguson, I., Lavalette, M. and Penketh, L. (2004) *Social work and social justice: A manifesto for a new engaged practice*, Social Work Future, https://socialworkfuture. org/2011/09/30/social-work-and-social-justice-a-manifesto-for-a-new-engaged-practice/ (Accessed 30 November 2018).

Jones, K. (2002) *Education in Britain: 1944 to the present*, London: Polity Press.

Kemmis, S., Wilkinson, J., Hardy, I. and Edwards-Groves, C. (2009) *Leading and learning: Developing ecologies of educational practice: Australian Association for Research in Education Symposium: Ecologies of practice.*

Kesby, M. (2007) Spatialising participatory approaches: the contribution of geography to a mature debate, *Environment and Planning A*, 39: 2813–2831.

King, L. and Grant, K. (2016) Meet social workers supporting refugees in Calais, *Community Care*, 24 August, http://www. communitycare.co.uk/2016/08/24/meet-social-workers-supporting-refugees-calais/

King, R. (2006) Analysing the Higher Education Regulatory State, *Discussion Paper No.38*, Centre for Analysis of Risk and Regulation, LSE, London.

King, R. (2007) *The regulatory state in an age of governance: Soft words and big sticks*, Basingstoke: Palgrave Macmillan.

Klein, R. (2014) *The "snowy white peaks" of the NHS: A survey of discrimination in governance and leadership and the potential impact on patient care in London and England*, Middlesex University Research Repository.

Kopola, N. (1997) Is the concept "active woman" an oxymoron in Hannah Arendt's *The Human Condition*, *NORA – Nordic Journal of Feminist and Gender Research*, 6(1): 48–58.

Kreber, C. (2015) The 'civic-minded' professional? An exploration through Hannah Arendt's '*vita activa*', *Educational Philosophy and Theory*, 48(2): 123–137.

Kuhlmann, E. and Saks, M. (2008) Health policy and workforce dynamics: the future, in E. Kuhlmann and M. Saks (eds) *Rethinking professional governance: International directions in healthcare*, Bristol: Policy Press: 235–44.

Lavalette, M. (2011) *Radical Social Work Today Social work at the crossroads*, Bristol: Policy Press.

Lawy, R.S. and Biesta, G.J.J. (2006) Citizenship-as-practice: the educational implications of an inclusive and relational understanding of citizenship, *British Journal of Educational Studies*, 54(1): 34–50.

Leeds City Council (2018) *Restorative Practice*, https://www.leeds.gov.uk/docs/Restorative%20Practice.pdf (Accessed 30 November 2018).

Le Grand, J. (2006*) Motivation, agency and public policy: Of knights and knaves, pawns and queens*, Oxford: Oxford University Press.

Lethbridge, E.J. (2015) *How public management reform influenced three professional groups – teachers, nurses and social workers – in England during the period 1979–2010*, A thesis submitted in partial fulfilment of the requirements of the University of Greenwich for the degree of Doctor of Philosophy, University of Greenwich.

Lethbridge J. (2018) Learning the lessons of Carillion, *Red Pepper*, 23 February.

Levi-Faur, D. (2013) The odyssey of the regulatory state: from a "thin" monomorphic concept to a "thick" and polymorphic concept, *Law and Policy*, 35(1–2): 29–50.

Leys, C. (1983) *Politics in Britain*, London: Heinemann Educational Books.

Leys, C. (2001) *Market-driven politics: Neoliberal democracy and the public interest*, London: Verso.

Lilo, E., Delaney, A., Blackwell, K. and Rapozo, D. (2015) *Good practice of promoting multi-disciplinary working with asylum seekers and refugees – The social work perspective* (5th edition), Liverpool: Mersey Care NHS Trust in Collaboration with Asylum Link Merseyside.

Lipsky, M. (1980) *Street-level bureaucracy dilemmas of the individual in public services*, New York: Russell Sage Foundations.

Loeffler, E. and Bovaird, T. (2016) User and community co-production of public services: what does the evidence tell us? *International Journal of Public Administration*, 39(13): 1006–1019.

London Edinburgh Weekend Return Group (1980) *In and against the state*, https://libcom.org/library/against-state-1979 (accessed 23 November 2018).

Lorenz, W. (2008) Paradigms and politics: understanding methods paradigms in an historical context: The case of social pedagogy, *British Journal of Social Work*, 38: 625–644.

Macintosh, M. (1996) Introduction to 'The public good', *Soundings*, 4: 104–109.

Maharg, P. (2009) *Associated life: Social software, professional relationships and democratic professionalism*, http://learningtobeprofessional.pbworks.com/w/page/15915004/Paul%20Maharg_(Accessed 30 November 2018).

Majone, G. (2010) *The transformation of the regulatory state*, Osservatorio sull'Analisi di Impatto della Regolazione, www.osservatorioair.it

Marshall, T.H. (1939) The recent history of professionalism in relation to social structure and social policy, *Canadian Journal of Economics and Political Science/Revue canadienne d'Economique et de Science politique*, 5(3): 325–340.

Matheson, A. (2002) Public sector modernisation: a new agenda, Paper prepared for the *26th Session of the Public Management Committee of the OECD*, Paris: 30–31 October.

Matten, D. and Crane, A. (2005) Corporate citizenship: towards an extended theoretical conceptualisation, *Academy of Management Review*, 30(1): 166–179.

Mayer, R.C., Davis, J.H. and Schoorman, F.D. (1995) An integrative model of organizational trust, *Academy of Management Review*, 20(3): 709–734.

Mayo, M., Hoggett, P. and Miller, S. (2007) Navigating the contradictions of public service modernisation: the case of community engagement professionals, *Policy and Politics*, 35(4): 667–681.

Mazzucatto, M. (2011) *The entrepreneurial state*, London: Demos.

McGregor-Smith R. (2017) *The time for talking is over, now is the time to act: Race in the workplace*, Assets Publishing Service UK Government.

McLaughlin, K., Osborne, S.P. and Ferlie, E. (2002) *New public management current trends and future prospects*, London: Routledge.

Moore, R. (2018) Forensic architecture: detail behind the devilry, *The Observer*, 25 February.

Moran, M. (2004) *The British Regulatory State: High Modernism and Hyper-Innovation*, London: Oxford University Press.

Morozov, E. (2015) Socialise the data centres, *New Left Review*, 91 (Jan/Feb): 45–66.

Naidoo, R. (2008) Building or eroding intellectual capital? Student consumerism as a cultural force in the context of knowledge economy, in J. Välimaa and O.-H. Ylijoki (eds), *Cultural Perspectives in Higher Education*, Netherlands: Springer: 43–55.

NASUWT (2011) Survey of members, NASUWT.

National Union of Teachers (NUT) (2015) *Vote for education: A manifesto for our children's education*, https://www.teachers.org. uk/parents (Accessed April 2015).

Neary, M. (1997) *Youth training and the training state: The real history of youth training in the twentieth century*, Basingstoke: Macmillan.

Neary, M. and Winn, J. (2009) The student as producer: reinventing the student experience in higher education, in L. Bell, M. Neary and H. Stevenson (eds), *The future of higher education: Policy, pedagogy and the student experience*, London: Continuum: 192–210.

Neary, M. and Winn, J. (2017) There is an alternative: A report on an action research project to develop a framework for co-operative higher education, *Learning and Teaching*, 10(1): 87–105.

Neave, G. (1998) The evaluative state reconsidered, *European Journal of Education*, 33(3): 265–284.

Neiman, M. and Stanborough, S.J. (1998) Rational choice theory and the evaluation of public policy, *Policy Studies Journal*, 26(3): 449–465.

New Economics Foundation (2013) *Framing the economy: The austerity story*, London: New Economics Foundation https://neweconomics.org/ (Accessed on 30 November 2018).

NICE (National Institute for Clinical and Public Health Excellence) (2014) *Developing NICE guidelines: the manual*, Process and methods guides London: NICE.

Oberhuemer, P. (2005) International perspectives on early childhood curricula, *International Journal of Early Childhood*, 37(1): 27–37.

O'Hara, G. (2012) *Governing post-war Britain: The paradoxes of progress, 1951–1973*, London: Palgrave Macmillan.

Olin Wright, E (2010) *Envisioning utopias*, London: Verso.

Osborne, D. and Gaebler, T. (1992) *Re-inventing government*, Reading, MA: Addison-Wesley Publishing Company.

Ostrom, E. (1972) Metropolitan reform: propositions derived from two traditions, *Social Science Quarterly*, 53: 474–493.

Ostrom, E. (1990) *Governing the commons: The evolution of institutions for collective action*, Cambridge: Cambridge University Press.

Ostrom, E. (2009) Design principles of robust property rights institutions: what have we learned? In G.K. Ingram and Y.-H. Hong (eds), *Property rights and land policies*, Cambridge, MA: Lincoln Institute of Land Policy: 25–51.

Papadimos, T.J. (2009) Reflective thinking and medical students: some thoughtful distillations regarding John Dewey and Hannah Arendt, *Philosophy, Ethics, and Humanities in Medicine*, 4(5), (Open access) https://peh-med.biomedcentral.com/articles/10.1186/1747-5341-4-5 (Accessed 25 November 2018).

Parsons, T. (1939) The professions and social structure, *Social forces*, 17(4): 457–467.

Pianalto, M. (2012) Integrity and struggle philosophia, *Philosophical Quarterly of Israel*, 40(2): 1–33.

Piore, M.J. (2011) Beyond markets: sociology, street-level bureaucracy, and the management of the public sector, *Regulation and Governance*, 5: 145–164.

Player, S. and Leys, C. (2010) *The plot against the NHS*, London: Merlin Press.

Pohl, C. Rist, S., Zimmermann, A., Fry, P., Gurung, G.S. et al (2010) Researchers' roles in knowledge production: experience from sustainability research in Kenya, Switzerland, Bolivia and Nepal, *Science and Public Policy*, 37(4): 267–281.

Polanyi, M. (1958) *Personal knowledge, towards a post-critical philosophy*, Chicago: University of Chicago Press.

Polanyi, M. (1966) *The tacit dimension*, London: Routledge and Kegan Paul Ltd.

Pollitt, C. and Bouckaert, G. (2004) *Public management reform: A comparative analysis*, London: Oxford University Press.

Radical Nurses Group (1981, 1988) *Newsletters January 1981 and Autumn 1988*, Royal College of Nursing Archives.

Ranson, S. (2018) *Education and democratic participation: The making of learning communities*, London: Routledge.

Red Quadrant/StreetDoctors (2015) *StreetDoctors final evaluation report*, December 2015.

Red Tecla (2018) *Presentacion*, http://www.redtecla.org/presentacion (Accessed 30 November 2018).

Rhodes, R.A.W. (1994) The hollowing out of the state, *Political Quarterly*, 65: 138–151.

Rhodes, R.A.W. (1997) *Understanding governance: Policy networks, governance, reflexivity and accountability*, Buckingham: Open University Press.

Rhodes, R.A.W. (2007) Understanding governance: ten years on, *Organization Studies*, 28(8): 1243–1264.

Rinaldi, C. (2004) The relationship between documentation and assessment, *The Quarterly Periodical of the North American Reggio Emilia Alliance*, 11(1): 1–4.

Royal College of Nursing (2017) *Safe and effective staffing survey: Nursing against the odds*, London: RCN.

Runnymede Trust (2014) *Why isn't my professor Black? On reflection*, Runnymede Trust Blog, https://www.runnymedetrust.org/blog/why-isnt-my-professor-black (Accessed 30 November 2018).

Rustin, S. (2017) We tried to cope hour by hour: the schools in shadow of Grenfell Tower, *The Guardian*, 27 November.

Sachs, J. (2001) Teacher professional identity: competing discourses, competing outcomes, *Journal of Education Policy*, 16(2): 149–161.

Sachs, J. (2003) *The activist teaching profession*, Maidenhead: Open University Press.

Sandlin, J., O'Malley, M.P. and Burdick, J. (2011) Mapping the complexity of public pedagogy scholarship 1894–2010, *Review of Educational Research*, 81(3): 338–375.

Scott, W.R. (2008) Lords of the dance: professionals as institutional agents, *Organizational Studies*, 29(2): 219–238.

Searle, C. (2017) *Isaac and I: A life in poetry*, Nottingham: Five Leaves.

Sefton-Green, J. (2013) *Learning at not-school: A review of study, theory and advocacy for education in non-formal settings*, John D. and Catherine T. MacArthur Foundation reports on digital medical and learning, MIT Press.

Silberman, S. (2015) *NeuroTribes: The legacy of autism and how to think smarter about people who think differently*, Australia/New Zealand: Allen and Unwin.

(The) Silent University (2012a) *The Silent University*, http://thesilentuniversity.org/ (Accessed 30 November 2018).

(The) Silent University (2012b) *The Silent University Reader* https://www.tate.org.uk/download/file/fid/30087 (Accessed 9 May 2019).

Simon, B. (1994) *State and educational change: Essays in the history of education and pedagogy*, London: Lawrence and Wishart.

Singleton, V. and Mee S. (2017) Critical compassion: affect, discretion and policy-care relations, *The Sociological Review Monographs*, 65(2): 130–149.

Sketcher, C. (2000) Changing images of the state: overloaded, hollowed-out, congested, *Public Policy and Administration*, 15(3): 1–19.

Social Work Action Network (SWAN) (2015) About SWAN, http://socialworkfuture.org/ (Accessed 30 November 2018).

Spours, K. (2014) *Education professionalism and New Times: An international and democratic model*, Presentation at Institute of Education, January.

Standing, G. (2011) *The precariat, the new dangerous class*, London: Bloomsbury Academic.

Standing, G (2014) *A precariat charter from denizens to citizens*, London: Bloomsbury Academic.

Stephen King Photography (2013) *The occupation of Croxteth Comprehensive School, 1982–1985*, http://www.stephenkingphotography.co.uk/croccy-comp (Accessed November 2018).

Stevenson, H. and Gilliland, A. (2015) The teachers' voice: teachers unions at the heart of new democratic professionalism, in J. Evers and R. Kneyber (eds) *Flip the system*, Geneva: Education International.

Steijn, B. (2002) HRM in the public sector: a neglected subject. Modernisation review – the HRM perspective, paper prepared for the *Human Resource Management Working Party Meeting* OECD headquarters, Paris 7–8 October.

Stiglitz, J. (2000) *Economics of the public sector*, New York: W.W. Norton and Co.

Streek W. (2016) *How will capitalism end?* London: Verso.

StreetDoctors (2018) *Who we are*, http://streetdoctors.org/who-we-are/

Sullivan, W.M. (2004) Can professionalism still be a viable ethic? *The Good Society*, Committee on the Political Economy of the Good Society, 13(1): 15–20.

Susskind, R. and Susskind, D. (2015) *The future of the professions how technology will transform the work of human experts*, Oxford: Oxford University Press.

Taubman, D. (2011) *Towards a progressive concept of professionalism*, Paper presented at Liverpool Community College, July.

Taubman, D. (2013) *Towards a UCU concept of professionalism*, Presentation for Towards a UCU Concept of Professionalism Conference, 20 March.

Tendler, J. (1997) *Good government in the Tropics*, Baltimore, MD: The John Hopkins University Press.

Thorpe, A. and Gamman, L. (2013) Learning together: students and community groups co-designing for carbon reduction in the London Borough of Camden, in E. Manzini and E. Staszowski (eds) *Public and collaborative: Exploring the intersection of design, social innovation and public policy*, DESIS Network: 51–75.

Todd, S. (2014) *The people, the rise and fall of the working class 1910–2010*, London: Murray.

Totschnig, W. (2017) Arendt's notion of natality an attempt at clarification, *Ideas y Valores*, 66(165): 327–346.

Tullock, G. (1965) *The politics of bureaucracy*, Washington: Public Affairs Press.

UK Government (2015) *Fulfilling our potential: Teaching excellence, social mobility and student choice*, Presented to Parliament by the Secretary of State for Business, Innovation and Skills, by Command of Her Majesty Cm9141, London: HM Government.

Unger, R. M. (2005) *What should the left propose?* London: Verso.

Van de Walle, S., Van Roostroek, S. and Boukaert, G. (2008) Trust in the public sector: is there evidence for a long-term decline? *International Review of Administrative Sciences*, 4(1): 47–64.

Van Eijk, C. and Steen, T. (2016) Why engage in co-production in public services? Mixing theory and empirical evidence, *International Review of Administrative Sciences*, 82(1): 28–46.

Ventres, W., Dharamsi, S. and Ferrer, R. (2016) From social determinants to social interdependency: Theory, reflection, and engagement, *Social Medicine*, 11(2): 84–89.

Wacjman, J. (1998) *Managing like a man: Women and men in corporate management*, Cambridge: Polity Press in association with Blackwell Publishers Ltd.

Wagenaar, H. (2007) Governance, complexity, and democratic participation: how citizens and public officials harness the complexities of neighbourhood decline, *The American Review of Public Administration*, 37(1): 17–50.

Wall, E. and Waterman, T. (2018) *Landscape and agency critical essays*, Abingdon: Routledge.

Weber, M. (1914) *Economy and society*, Routledge Revivals.

Weber, M. (1948) *From Max Weber: Essays in sociology*, The International Library of Sociology and Social Reconstruction, London: Routledge and Kegan Paul.

Weik, E. (2012) Introducing "The creativity of action" into institutionalist theory, *M@n@gement*, 15(5): 563–581.

Whitty, G. (2000) Teacher professionalism in New Times, *Journal of In-Service Education*, 26(2): 281–295.

References

Whitty, G. and Wisby, E. (2006) Moving beyond recent educational reform and towards democratic professionalism, *Hitotsubashi Journal of Social Studies*, 38: 43–61.

Winfield, L. (2016) An example of co-production – LYPFT's Multi Agency Clinical Risk Training Project, https://coproductionblog.wordpress.com/2017/08/15/an-example-of-co-production-lypfts-multi-agency-clinical-risk-training-project-by-leanne-winfield/

Williams, R. (1976) *Key words*, London: Penguin.

Wolff, J. (2018) Agency, advocacy, vocabulary, three landscape projects, in E. Wall and T. Waterman (eds) *Landscape and agency critical essays*, Abingdon: Routledge.

Wrede, S. (2008) Unpacking gendered professional power in the welfare state, *Equal Opportunities International*, 27(1): 19–33.

Zafirovski, M. (2001) Administration and society: beyond public choice? *Public Administration*, 79(3): 665–688.

179

Index

Royal College of Nursing (RCN)
22–3
S
schools
Croxteth School 103–4, 142
response to Grenfell fire 131–3,
143
Stepney School 97–8, 144, 149
see also education; teachers
science 59–60
Scott, W.R. 32
Searle, Chris 97–8, 144, 149
service user-professional relationship
democratic examples 103–7
impact of reforms on 118–19,
137–8
listening and knowledge-sharing
96–8
models of 92–5
service users
expertise of 57, 58, 60, 64–7,
69–73, 74–5, 148–9
family expertise 69–73, 148
role of 90, 158
see also co-production;
communities
Sickle Cell and Thalassemia Centre
101
Silent University 81–2, 146, 149,
152
skills 55–6, 73–5
see also expertise; training and
development
social care, privatisation of 17, 88
social changes 14–15
social citizenship 35
social democratic welfare systems
37–8
social housing 122–4, 143
social interdependency approach
99–100
Social Science Centre (SSC) 79–81
social welfare 15, 65
Social Work Action Network
(SWAN) 90–1, 141
Social Work First 108–9
social work manifestos 90–1
social work and workers *153*
and expertise 65–6, 119–20

family expertise in Leeds 69–71,
145, 148, 150, 151
and freedom 89
impact of reforms on 23–4
international solidarity 108–9
Liverpool handbook for 106–7,
142–3, 149
and reflection 146–7
responses to democratic
professionalism 154
risk assessment 73–5, 145
training and development 151–2
Social Workers Without Borders
(SSWB) 108, 143, 149, 151
socially responsive design 76
space 70–1
see also public space
specialist tacit knowledge 58–9, 67
speech 48–9
SSC (Social Science Centre) 79–81
stakeholder democracy 117–18
stakeholders 60, 64–5, 103–4, 155
see also service users
state
changing role of 15–17, 39–44
and professionals 30–9
see also public sector reforms
Steen, T. 11–12
Steijn, B. 20
'Stepney Words' 97–8, 144, 149
Stepwise programme 125
Stevenson, H. 97
street level bureaucrats 92–4
StreetDoctors 124–5, 143, 151
structuration theory 32–3
'Student as Producer' 79, 142, 148
Sullivan, W.M. 7
supervision of social workers 23
support, for democratic
professionalism 154–7
Susskind, D. 62
Susskind, R. 62
T
Taubman, D. 8–9, *52*
teachers
impact of reforms on 21–2
response to Grenfell Tower fire
131–3
responsibility of 7–8, 119